Fighting Back

Fighting Back

A LIFE IN THE STRUGGLE FOR CIVIL RIGHTS

From oral history interviews with Dr. James B. McMillan
conducted by Gary E. Elliott
a narrative interpretation by R. T. King

University of Nevada Oral History Program

Publication of *Fighting Back* was made possible in part
by gifts from Robert D. Faiss and the John Ben Snow Trust.

Copyright 1997
University of Nevada Oral History Program
Reno, Nevada 89557

Library of Congress Cataloging-in-Publication Data:

King, R. T. (Robert Thomas), 1944-
    Fighting back : a life in the struggle for civil rights / from oral
history interviews with Dr. James B. McMillan ; conducted by Gary E.
Elliott ; a narrative interpretation by R.T. King.
        p.   cm.
    Includes index.
    ISBN 1-56475-374-3 (cloth)
    1. McMillan, James B., 1917-   . 2. Afro-American civil rights
workers—Nevada—Las Vegas—Biography. 3. Civil rights workers—
Nevada—Las Vegas—Biography. 4. Afro-Americans—Segregation—
Nevada—Las Vegas—History—20th century. 5. Las Vegas (Nev.)—
Race relations. 6. Civil rights movements—Nevada—Las Vegas—
History—20th century. I. Elliott, Gary, 1941-   . II. McMillan,
James B., 1917-   . III. Title.
F849.L35K56   1997
979.3'135—dc21   97-38446
                                                        CIP

Publication Staff:
Production Manager: Kathleen M. Coles
Production Assistants: Danny K. Howard, Linda J. Sommer
Jacket Photo by Dave Duarte

Contents

Preface

T HROUGH TAPE-RECORDED interviews of people with historically significant experiences, the University of Nevada Oral History Program (UNOHP) is exploring the remembered past. The program's 60,000 page collection of transcripts is rich in information about the twentieth-century history of Nevada and the American West, presented in a way that captures the human dimension which is so often absent from other forms of documentation. In addition to its transcripts, which are heavily used by researchers, the UNOHP occasionally publishes refined, narrative interpretations of oral histories selected for the depth of their contents and the breadth of their appeal to general readers. *Fighting Back* is the most recent of these.

The African-American population of Nevada was statistically insignificant prior to World War II, when large numbers of Southern blacks moved to Clark County seeking employment in war industries such as Basic Magnesium, Incorporated. Most were segregated into an outlying area of Las Vegas which came to be known as the Westside. They were not inclined to accept second-class citizen status. Some began an effort to secure their civil rights, and by the 1950s they were taking organized, collective action. In 1986 the UNOHP conducted an oral history with Lubertha Johnson, who was an early arrival on the Westside and who became a leader of the community. Mrs. Johnson's was the first in a series of oral histories that are intended to document two linked subjects: the history of the Westside, and the African-American struggle for civil rights in Nevada. To date six other oral histories have been completed on these subjects. *Fighting Back* arises from one of them.

Between December of 1993 and August 1995, Dr. Gary E. Elliott, a historian on the faculty of the Community College of Southern Nevada, conducted sixteen hours of oral history interviews with Dr. James B. McMillan and his wife, Marie. This book is crafted from the 600-page verbatim transcript of those interviews. Remaining faithful to their contents, and adhering as closely as possible to the McMillans' spoken words, I have composed the narrative published as *Fighting Back*. The McMillans have reviewed my work and affirmed that it is an accurate interpretation. Readers who desire access to the unaltered oral history are invited to visit the offices of the UNOHP, where the tapes of the interviews may be heard by appointment.

As with all of its oral histories, while the UNOHP can vouch for the authenticity of *Fighting Back*, it makes no claim that the recollections upon which the book is based are entirely free of error. This is personal history; this is the past as remembered by James and Marie McMillan. It is also a powerful story that reveals much about human nature and race relations in twentieth-century America.

R. T. KING
University of Nevada

Introduction

JAMES B. McMILLAN was born in 1917 in a small town in racially segregated Mississippi. In that year the U.S. Supreme Court ruled that ordinances compelling residential segregation of the races were in violation of the Fourteenth Amendment. Gradually, over the next five decades, most of the legal foundation of racial discrimination in America was brought down, but McMillan's life is confirmation of C. Vann Woodward's observation that "there was more Jim Crowism than Jim Crow laws."

In 1922 James McMillan's mother took her child and joined the swelling flood of blacks migrating to Northern industrial cities. They were fleeing continued segregation, violence, and the knowledge that African-Americans remained outside the protection of the law in the South. Moving first to New York, then to Philadelphia, to Detroit, and finally to a relatively stable life in Hamtramck, Michigan, the two experienced poverty, racism, and de facto segregation everywhere. They were also introduced to the color-blind power of political patronage, and to the economic opportunities of illegal enterprise for those shut out of the mainstream economy.

McMillan learned from his mother to be outspoken and to work hard in school (he was always better at the former than the latter), and in high school he became a reasonably good student and an outstanding athlete. He was awarded an athletic scholarship to the University of Detroit, where he was the only black on the football team; but in his junior year, for reasons associated with race, he lost the scholarship and could afford to continue his studies only by working full time in an automobile factory. Persevering, he went on to earn a degree from Meharry Medical College's School of Dentistry in 1944.

Following service in the U. S. Army in World War II McMillan started a dental practice in Detroit. He was recalled to service at the end of the Korean War. After being discharged, he and his wife relocated to Las Vegas. McMillan liked Las Vegas from the beginning—it was a twenty-four hour town, with lots of live entertainment, gambling, sunshine, and money—but he encountered the same types of racial discrimination there that he had lived with all of his life. He would not put up with it. Within a year of his arrival he was speaking out and attacking segregation in Las Vegas with such passion and vehemence that he was elected president of the local branch of the NAACP. Under his leadership, and following the example of civil rights activists in the South, the branch was soon taking direct, confrontational action to end overt segregation in Las Vegas; and in 1960, end it they did, in dramatic and surprising fashion.

Fighting Back is James B. McMillan's memoir of a life spent fighting racial discrimination in its many forms.

His story is personal, but it is representative of the experiences of thousands of other African-Americans who struggled to transform the Constitution from a document concerned primarily with property rights and federalism into a charter for equality. Although the fuse had long been smoldering, the black Americans who took to the streets in 1960 ignited a legal and constitutional revolution that eventually benefitted all disadvantaged groups in American society.

As the doors to full participation slowly began to open, many African-Americans who had marched for civil rights in the late 1950s and early 1960s sought new ways to advance the cause of racial equality. McMillan stepped down as president of the Las Vegas NAACP in 1961, but for over forty years he has continued to speak for the interests of the black community. He was appointed to the State Board of Dental Examiners, the Board of Directors of Health Plan of Nevada, and the Economic Opportunity Board Health Committee; and he served as a member of the Small Business Administration Advisory Council, chairman of the Governor's Commission on Minority Business Enterprises, member of the Board of Directors and Editorial Board of KVBC Television, and director of the Clark County Boys' Club. McMillan even ventured into election politics. He was too outspoken to have much success, but in 1992 he was elected to the non-partisan Clark County School Board, and for the next four years he spent his free evenings and weekends poring over the mountain of paperwork associated with school board affairs.

From start to finish it took almost four years to complete the project which has led to this book. During that time I got to know Dr. James B. McMillan well, to respect him, and to admire what he has done with his life. His friends call him "Mac"; I call him Mac too, because it seems natural to do so, and I hope he counts me among his friends. What I like most about Mac is that his approach to life is the antithesis of what is commonly referred to today as "politically correct." He would be more at home among professed bigots, arguing against their stereotypes and fallacies, than in the company of polite society with its thinly disguised petty politics and hollow conversation.

Although McMillan acknowledges that since the 1950s tremendous progress has been made toward what his wife Marie calls his great passion—"the betterment of his people"—he worries that those gains will be wiped away by a rising tide of conservative reaction similar to the one that doomed the first reconstruction era. His unwavering support for affirmative action and majority-minority voting districts is a reflection of that concern. Mac has made a few concessions to age (he walks slower and has less energy) but the fire still burns. He is always up for a good argument, and we have had a few, always good natured; but as in 1960, Mac will not back down when the issue is equality—and the struggle continues.

GARY E. ELLIOTT
Community College of Southern Nevada

1

Mother Was My Closest Companion

GRANDMOTHER OPHELIA REDMAN came out of slavery in the West Indies and somehow made her way to Aberdeen, Mississippi, where she met and married Sam Gay, a white veterinarian who had a big farm or plantation . . . . Well, they weren't really married, I guess: my grandmother was Sam Gay's concubine. But their relationship wasn't a secret—she lived on his land and she took his name, and the three children from their marriage lived with her. My mother, their only daughter, was born on April 27, 1896. They named her Rosalie.

After Mr. Gay had these children with my grandmother he married a young white woman and produced another family of three girls; but it was public knowledge in Aberdeen that my mother and her brothers were Old Man Gay's children, and he protected them all his life— as long as he was living they didn't have any worry about trouble from whites. Mr. Gay was about six feet three

inches tall, with the typical sharp face of a white southerner, what we'd call a "cracker." Some of my earliest
memories are of him coming to visit—he'd ride up on his
white horse with his boots shined, tie the horse to the
post and just step over the fence, he was so tall. I'd be
playing in the yard, and he'd pick me up and carry me
into the house where he and my mother would sit and
talk awhile; then he'd leave.

Old Man Gay had given our family almost three
hundred acres of land, but when my mother and I later
left Mississippi no one continued paying taxes on it, and
we lost it. There were other caucasian men who took care
of their black concubines and their children that way. My
mother told me about a relative in Mississippi who lived
with a caucasian who had six or seven hundred acres of
land, and they had four or five children. As those children grew up, he gave each of them some of his land
according to the way that they married. When one of his
girls married a real light man, he gave her maybe a
hundred acres of the land; but when one of his boys
married a real dark girl who was clearly negro, he gave
him only twenty-five or thirty acres. You didn't want to
be too dark.

My father, James Milton McMillan, was born in West
Virginia. He taught some school there, then traveled to
Mississippi and became a farm laborer—cotton, peanuts,
other crops. His marriage to my mother was his second,
and his son, Theodore McMillan, was my half brother. I
was born January 14, 1917. My father died during the
great flu epidemic of 1918, so I don't remember him, but
Mother would always tell me that he was a very neat and
orderly man. After I got older—sixteen, seventeen,

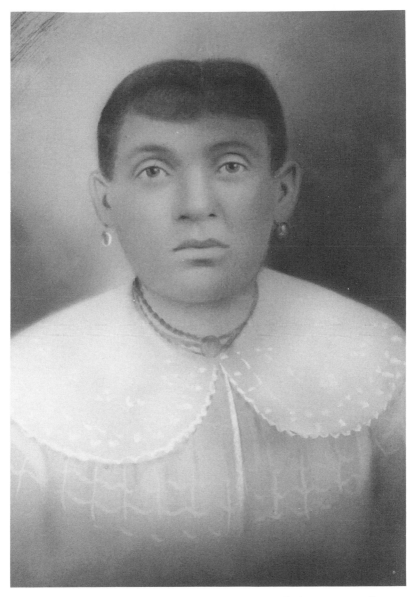

"Grandmother Ophelia Redman came out of slavery . . . ."

eighteen years old—she would say, "Your shoes aren't shined and you don't take care of yourself and you don't dress well. Your father would really have jumped on you, young man! You should be glad he isn't here."

Our house sat up on a little knoll in Aberdeen, and you could look down from it into the center of town. Grandmother Ophelia lived with us. When she came down with pneumonia, they put one of those tent-type things over her bed and put steam under it so she could get enough air in her lungs, and that's the way she died. I remember her dying, but not complaining—she was just there in the bed, under the tent, and I'd be in the room with her; I'd come in and watch her. She lived about a week and then she died.

Behind our place there was a gambling joint, and on weekends caucasians used to walk through our yard to get to it—I'd be in the back yard playing, and they'd walk through and go into this gambling house. Later my mother would find coins in my pocket—she just didn't understand where that money was coming from. She told me that one day when I was out playing she saw these white men come through the back yard and rub my head and put some money in my pocket, so she went out there and said, "What are you doing to my child?" They said, "Oh, nothing, Rosalie. We're just rubbing his head for luck and putting some money in his pocket." Rubbing the little black boy's head for luck . . . this wasn't unusual in the South.

My mother was outspoken and proud. She was very light skinned, and since she was Sam Gay's daughter she thought that she didn't have to kowtow to any of the caucasians or to the customs of segregation in Mississippi. She would go anywhere she wanted, such as downtown shopping or what have you; but when my grandfather Gay went blind shortly before he died, he couldn't protect her anymore, and she got into some trouble downtown with a caucasian man and woman. They called her "nigger" and other names and hit her. She hit back. A couple of days later white men came to our house in Ku Klux Klan robes, with their faces covered. They took my mother out and tied her to a post downtown; stripped her blouse off and gave her fifteen lashes across her back with a whip. From the front porch of our house on the hill I could look down and see this. I couldn't understand why it was happening to my mother, but there was nothing I could do, and I just cried. Then some people brought my mother home—she was crying and angry and her back was bleeding. I was five years old.

In the next few weeks my mother got well, but she'd decided that we would get out of Mississippi, get out of the South. Trains to New York, Chicago, or St. Louis were the three main routes that black people took going north, and I can remember being all dressed up and going to the train station, where there was a big engine with steam popping out. We got on the train to New York, and when we got there, New York was where we stayed, just my mother and I. It was a one-parent family.

My birth certificate says that my mother was a domestic, but she'd gone to school, and she was a practical nurse. She could also sew, and she got work as a seamstress in garment factories in New York—that's how she made a living. We had a little apartment in Harlem, and at first she'd leave me with people when she would go to do sewing in the factories. As I got older, I would walk to school and she'd go to work, and in the evening I'd be back home waiting for her to come home from the garment factory.

I was still quite young when we moved again. My mother was interested in getting married, and she'd met a gentleman and they'd started dating and going together. He wanted to go to Philadelphia, so we left and moved there. He'd fought in World War I, winning a medal in the Battle of the Argonne Forest, and he was quite a guy. In Philadelphia my mother and her man were just kind of living together, they weren't married, so she sent me to a Catholic boarding school for a year. At night the nuns would read to us—*Robin Hood* and all of these different stories. (I'd never had that in my home. My mother had to spend her time pacifying her man and she didn't read to me.) Soon I almost had those stories committed to memory. When I came back things were pretty good at first, but my father . . . well, he wasn't my father—this *gentleman* got busted for making bathtub whiskey. You could smell the mash all over the neighborhood, and he got busted. That really upset my mother.

We had a nice little house, but my mother never did marry this guy. They broke up over the episode with the whiskey, and after Mother separated from him we moved to another black neighborhood. Philadelphia was really a segregated town: when I was eight years old I was working on a milk truck with a white fellow, and he would leave me outside the gate of the big Girard Boarding School when he went in to deliver milk to it. Not only could blacks not go to that school, they couldn't even set foot on the campus.

My mother had joined the Catholic church when she left Mississippi, and I can remember us going to church every Sunday. When I was seven or eight years old she wanted to make me an altar boy. I tried, but I'd rather fool around with the other guys back behind the church—we used to steal wine out of the sacristy and drink it with the guys out back. My mother went to church every Sunday, all the holidays, but she wasn't a fanatic with religion. She was just a good woman who believed in promises, and she practiced her faith and made me practice it.

Eventually, when I was about ten years old, my mother married a man named Emery Philpot. Mr. Philpot was from North Carolina, and he'd been raised by white people, Quakers. He was a real stern, ethical man. When we ate breakfast everybody sat down to the table; everybody had to be home and eat dinner together after work; and he demanded certain things and types of behavior from me. My mother seemed to be very happy with him, and she shared many of his views. She was an ethical woman who was true to her word, and she raised me to be that way.

My mother didn't drink strong alcohol, but she'd have a glass of wine. My stepfather did drink whiskey, and he participated in gambling, a game they called "numbers." But he would always make sure that he had a job. He was a cement finisher, what they called Gunite—a mixture of cement, sand and water that would be blown onto buildings through high pressure hoses.

"We had a nice house and I was going to school . . . ."
James B. McMillan, Philadelphia, Easter, 1926.

He'd be up on the scaffold with that big hose working on those tall buildings in downtown Philadelphia.

My mother was my closest companion as I grew up, and she taught me things like how to dance and how to ride horses, but our family life really started with her marriage to Mr. Philpot. We had a nice house, and I was going to school; and my mother bought a piano, and I took piano lessons. She always impressed upon me the need for an education. The weak point in my education was that she didn't have time to spend an hour or so with me every day on school work because she had to work and make a living, and she had to keep the family happy. I was kind of a tough kid for her to keep in shape, but she did—she was a strict disciplinarian. I had to conduct myself decently and act properly. My stepfather was a disciplinarian also, but my mother wouldn't let him spank me. She made it a rule that, "If anything happens and my son has to be disciplined, let me know and I will do it." And she did.

2

My Dad Had His Numbers Routes

IN THE 1920s HENRY FORD had recruited blacks throughout the South to come to Michigan to work in his automobile factory for two dollars and fifty cents a day. (He later raised that to five dollars a day.) My mother's brother, Dunbar Gay, and her half-sister, Nancy Tymms, moved to Michigan to get jobs and raise their families. Then in the midst of the Depression my stepfather found himself out of work, and we moved to Pontiac, Michigan, to stay with Aunt Nancy. My mother could almost have passed for white, but Aunt Nancy was Afro-American to the greatest. She was a child that my grandmother had had in a marriage with a black man. Uncle Dunbar, however, looked exactly like his father, Master Gay: he had blue eyes and blond hair, and even though he wasn't trying to pass, no one could tell him from a white man. (My uncle Sam Gay, named for his father, had stayed in Mississippi. He could pass for white too, but he got in trouble. A white man knew of his

background and called him a nigger; then they got in a
fight, and he killed the guy and left Mississippi and went
to Alabama to hide.) Uncle Dunbar had a job in the
Fisher body plant, where they would design automobiles
and stuff. He kept that job for thirty years. He was a
good worker, but when Friday came he would stop by
the liquor store, buy a quart of whiskey, and be drunk
Friday night, Saturday, and Sunday until five o'clock.
Monday he was sober and worked his five days and never
missed a day.

We lived with my Aunt Nancy's family in Pontiac for
three or four months, and when we ran out of money we
gave our piano to my aunt to help pay our bill. From
there we moved to Detroit. My stepfather figured he
could find some construction work, but he couldn't, so
we moved to Hamtramck, where we got a one bedroom
apartment with no bathtub and an outdoor toilet, and
my stepfather continued looking for a job. For weeks we
were on welfare, which is what they'd call the Red Cross
at that time. They were giving out rice and beans and
maybe some butter, and my dad would have to go stand
in line to get this so we could eat. He soon got tired of it
and embarrassed, and he says, "I'm not going to do this
anymore." So he became a numbers runner.

In New York, gangsters used to run illegal gambling
games called the "numbers." They didn't have the
numbers in Detroit; instead they had what they called
"policy," which was different. (Policy was like keno is in
Nevada—they would pull twelve numbers out of a basket
and write them on a slip of paper.) While he was on
welfare Dad met a black guy named Buddy Charity who
had a policy thing going, and Dad said, "Hey, man, we

can do better than this. Why don't we do the numbers like in New York?" Buddy Charity drove a green Cadillac, wore a derby hat, and smoked cigars, and he weighed about two hundred and sixty pounds—he looked like Andy in the "Amos and Andy" show. He was a wheeler and a dealer, and he got with the mob and started this numbers racket with my dad.

As a runner, my dad would go around from house to house in Hamtramck, telling people, "Hey, here's a book. Why don't you write some numbers?" He'd get ten cents for every dollar he took to the big fellows that backed the numbers, and he made a good living. He was soon doing so well that we moved into a house down the block. This was a *real* house. It had a living room, two bedrooms, a kitchen, and a backyard. We bought an Atwater Kent radio, and evenings the family would sit around the radio in the front room and listen to "The Lone Ranger," "Jack Benny," and all of those old programs.

Mother was religious, but she didn't disapprove of my dad running numbers.* She'd say, "Well, you know, we got to make a living." But I kept telling her, "I don't see why he has to take all this money and give it to someone else. He ought to back these numbers himself." She'd say, "No, that's too risky. We can't do that." But they could expand what they were already doing. One

---

*Especially in northern cities, the "numbers" or "policy" rackets offered blacks access to social prestige and economic opportunity equivalent to that enjoyed by the professional class. It has been estimated that in Chicago in the 1930s, there were as many blacks employed as numbers writers, runners, clerks and checkers as there were African-American doctors, lawyers, dentists, teachers and social workers. Numbers or policy kings often became community leaders who exerted political influence and supported philanthropic causes.

day they drove out of Hamtramck with Buddy Charity
and me in his Cadillac, and we went to Pontiac and
started another numbers route there. All of my family in
Pontiac were strong Baptists, "Holy Rollers," and a
couple of them were preachers. My mother contacted a
preacher who was a relative, gave him a book and
started him writing numbers. So the preacher is running
numbers for us, and he's turning two thousand dollars a
day. He'd never seen so much money, and he got in
trouble—he decided that he was going to bank it himself
one day, and he had a hit, and he couldn't pay off. So he
lost that big book.

When my dad had his numbers routes he used to go
to Pontiac (it was about thirty miles) and pick up all this
money and bring it back to Hamtramck. He was making
a lot of money. During the Depression he was making a
tremendous amount of money. But he was drinking
pretty heavy, too, like my Uncle Dunbar. He'd take a
fifth of whiskey when he was picking up these numbers,
and sip on it all day long and not really get drunk. And
he liked women and spent money on them, playing
around. He liked to gamble too. He'd go to the pool
rooms and shoot craps with those guys. Sometimes they'd
beat him out of his money; sometimes he'd bust them
and then pass their money back around, and they'd start
the game again so he didn't have to go home. And he'd
actually *give* his numbers money away—meet some poor
guy on the street, didn't have any money, and he'd say,
"Here's a hundred dollars. Do something for yourself."
My dad just squandered that numbers money. Still,
we got so affluent on what he brought home that when I

was in high school my family bought a house in a white neighborhood, on Carpenter Avenue up in the northern part of Hamtramck. I was working in the Plymouth Motor Car Company then, and the day we moved I left for work from our segregated neighborhood on Denton Avenue. While I was at work my family moved into the new house. My mother and my stepfather being light complexioned, I guess the neighbors didn't really know what race they were when they moved in; and when I came home that night from the factory to our new house, I walked through the neighborhood and it caused a little stir. People stared at me as if they wanted to know what this black kid was doing there. That was a Friday, the last day of work. Saturday someone had written on our house, "Niggers, move out!" Mother was furious and I was too.

We were the only black family for fifteen or twenty blocks around. My mother had found this house through a white councilman from Hamtramck who lived on the street. She had worked for him in a political campaign, so he knew us well. Shortly after we moved in he came to our house to let people know that he knew us, I guess, and as a sanction to let us live there and not to cause any disturbance. But I had already fought with the Polish kid next door—I had to give him a black eye to let him know we would not tolerate anything like the words that had been written on our house. It was our house, and they could respect the fact that we lived there and stay away from our property.

We were doing so well on my dad's numbers thing that we had two cars: we had a Chrysler, and by then I

was in high school and had an old Model A Ford. And
Mother was already into politics. She'd gotten involved
when we were still living in the ghetto on Denton
Avenue. She used to hold Democratic Party precinct
meetings at our house, and that led to a job for her as a
clerk in the city welfare department—her man had won.
It's a good thing she had this job, because in 1937, after
making all this money, my dad finally got caught. He
was working with the Purple Gang at the time, and the
FBI had been following him for a long time, which he
didn't know. We had bought this house, and I thought
that we were top middle class people. My mother did too.
It just got the best of her when they found out that she
was working in the numbers with my father.

When the FBI caught my dad and took him to court,
they had all the books in the house that they'd raided.
They knew how much money my dad's route was
producing, and it came out in court, and my mother was
sitting there listening. She got madder than hell when she
learned that his business was producing about thirteen
hundred dollars a week. He'd been giving her two
hundred a week, and she was working as a clerk in the
welfare department and had gotten raises to a hundred
dollars a week, so she was getting three hundred dollars
a week, and that was big time. We had new cars and this
house and furniture, and we had put central heating in.
We were living high and mighty, and my mother had
been satisfied that we were doing real good until she
found out just how well we *should* have been doing.

My stepdad owed Internal Revenue a lot of money,
but they just convicted him and dismissed him. There
wasn't any point in pursuing him for back taxes and

"My mother had been satisfied that we were doing real good until she found out how well we *should* have been doing."

fines—he probably owed fifty thousand dollars in income taxes, but we didn't know anything about income tax at that time. When he came home after they released him my mother was so angry with him that she told him, "Get out of this house! You've been making enough money for the last three or four years for us to be wealthy, to have a home on Boston Boulevard, for my son to be going to college, for us to have everything we want."

3

Becoming Somebody

WHEN WE FIRST MOVED to Hamtramck we lived in a segregated neighborhood. In fact, all housing was segregated in the Detroit area. Even Dearborn had always been a racist town—although Henry Ford sent recruiters to the South to bring blacks up to work in his plant, he had no housing for them that was not segregated. A lot of black auto workers moved to places like Hamtramck and Highland Park, but those were all segregated communities too. White people in the Detroit area simply didn't want blacks to live in their neighborhoods, and you couldn't go to court to make them—there was nothing you could do to force these people to let you live in decent housing. Blacks had to live in crowded, rundown old duplexes and fourplexes and cold-water flats.[*]

In grade school I would hang out with the other black kids. We had something in common, the same dialect and what have you, and you figured that if white kids were going to jump you, you'd have your buddies. All us black guys hung out together, and we got into a lot of fights and had a lot of disciplining. There was this guy they called Black John, and we were buddies. One day when we were on the playground he was going to fight, but the other guy said, "Well, I'm not going to fight you. You have a knife in your pocket. You'll cut me." So Black John took his knife out and threw it to me. I opened the blade and I'm standing there with the knife while they're fighting, and the principal sees me. He took me into his office and spanked me. The next day he called my mother in to see him, and he told her about the trouble I'd been in and what he'd done about it. She said, "Don't you ever spank my kid again. Call me and I'll do the necessary business," and she took me across her knee and spanked the hell out of me right in front of him. Then she took me home and spanked me again. She said, "I want you to be in school, and I want you to follow the rules and regulations and study. Don't you ever let me hear about you doing these things again."

---

[*]In the 1917 case of *Buchanan* v. *Warley* the United States Supreme Court had ruled that municipal ordinances prohibiting blacks from moving into white neighborhoods were unconstitutional. However, private agreements were not covered by the court's ruling, and the practice of establishing and preserving racially segregated neighborhoods remained widespread even in parts of the country that prided themselves on their racial tolerance.

I hung out with the black kids, and I talked their talk, but when I came home I tried to speak well. I also tried to be a good student; but I wasn't, and the teachers knew that I was a trouble maker. I got in trouble with my music teacher. She was having me sing "Do, re, mi . . . " and I couldn't. She thought I was acting up, thought I was being smart, and she put me out of the class; she put me into a little room by myself for that period for the rest of the term, and I learned how to do basket weaving and pottery in that room. Half a semester of baskets and pottery!

My education in the ghetto schools in Philadelphia had been very poor, and in first through fourth grades I had missed out on a lot. We spoke the English language, but we weren't learning to spell, to build a vocabulary, or to write well. Early on after we moved to Hamtramck, I realized that I had to get some type of learning. I knew what my deficiencies were and I learned how to compete within the system. In grade school I tried to spell; I'd go off to a spelling bee and I'd get bumped out when I misspelled a word, but that was OK—I would commit the word to memory. I knew that I had to learn the multiplication tables, so I sat down one Saturday and memorized them so that I would remember them the rest of my life. (My dad didn't have an education, and he was working in the numbers. He could do percentages; he knew how much money he had coming. I didn't realize it was just moving the decimal point, but he could do that.)

I learned to work within the system. I did well in geometry and history and things that I could commit to memory, and I had a terrific geometry teacher. She taught me to know the rules, to memorize them. And I did: I knew every rule that we had to know in geometry, and I got A's in it. When I moved on to high school we had a deal where you could take a test to get a C in the course and then you could do extra work for a B and extra work for an A. I did that, and when I finished high school I had a B average even though I was an athlete, because I'd learned how to use the system. Later in college I would still try to figure out the system. I studied the professor; I knew what he liked and what he didn't like, and I knew what lecture notes I had to take. I took two semesters of German and got a C+, but I couldn't speak a word of German. It's just knowing the system.

We didn't have a junior high school—we would go through the eighth grade in primary school, and then over to the high school to start the ninth grade. In the ninth grade I continued to be a ruffian. There was a white kid, a Polish kid named Kowalski, whose father owned a factory or something, and Kowalski would wear blue serge suits and white shirts and ties and stuff. I couldn't stand him. We'd fought all through grade school, and it continued in high school. One day in geometry the teacher called Kowalski up to the black-board. As he passed me I thought, "Here's this blue serge suit; here's this eraser with white chalk on it." I picked up the eraser and hit him on the butt, and then we started swinging at each other. The teacher grabbed me and said, "I know you, McMillan. My sister told me about you." (Her sister taught at the grammar school I'd come from.) "You're going down to see the principal."

It was the first time I was in trouble in high school. Not much came of it, but I knew I couldn't go on like this. I began to think about what I wanted to be. I saw all of these other kids that were big in school, and I saw the discipline of the school, and I said, "I've got to do something. I just can't be in this school and not be somebody." The night after my fight with Kowalski I went to a football rally. There was a black kid who played football; he was six two and he weighed over two hundred pounds and he was muscular. He was the star of the team. All the girls would put their arms around him and kiss him, and they sang these songs and had bonfires and everything, and I thought, "That's what I want to be. That's going to be my role in this high school."

I decided to change my way of acting, go out for athletics and take a college prep course. I knew that I could get a scholarship to college by playing football and running track, so that's what I set out to do. Also, athletics made me somebody in the community. I was happy with it; people knew me. And probably my love of athletics spurred me to do other things, because I knew that there were no black professional athletes. Blacks weren't making any money in sports, so after college I would have to do something else to make a living. I had to become a teacher or doctor or lawyer or an undertaker to make some money and be "respectable." Those were the only professions that were open to blacks at that time. (My mother had absolutely put her foot down—I was not going to be involved in the numbers or in the rackets.)

I had never played football, but I made the team in my freshman year, and eventually I made All State and All City playing end—at that time we played both ways, defense and offense. (This other black kid had played left end, so I played left end also.) I developed into a star on the football team and a star on the track team, setting city and state records in track. I won letters in all sports all four years. I won more letters, I guess, than anybody in the school, but in my junior year I hurt my rotator cuff and had to have an operation on my shoulder. When football season came around in the fall I could barely lift my arm. They put me in and let me play even though they figured I couldn't live up to my reputation, but I did—I ended my high school football career by catching a pass one handed with twenty-six seconds to go to win the championship game.

We had football banquets every year. The year before, a caucasian boy, a co-captain, had gotten up and spoken so well that the superintendent of schools said, "I withdraw my speech, because you really make mine look second class. I want to congratulate you." To me that was a great accomplishment, so the next semester I took public speaking and I learned how to give speeches. My senior year I was a co-captain, and our other co-captain was a Polish guy who couldn't talk or speak at all. That left me to make the speech at the banquet. My thing was to duplicate the young man who had spoken the year before, and to make the superintendent say the same thing that he had said to him. And I did.

Back then teachers weren't any easier on you just because you were an athlete, and I wanted to play so bad that I made myself study, just to make sure that I stayed eligible. That gave me focus. I got all my assignments in on time and made sure that I studied enough to get a C or better. Then I'd work toward a B, then an A. I was able to get a good education, and when I graduated one of the scholarships I got was for being the athlete with the highest grades.

About a third of our high school graduating class was black. We had a little integration, but there was also a lot of prejudice. My buddy George Jackson and I kind of hung out together—there was a corner where all the black kids hung out, and we had to protect our turf. We had fights with Polish kids until they respected us and we respected them, and then we got to be buddies . . . or at least we tolerated each other. George and I would sometimes take the streetcar and go downtown with some girls from our school. Being athletes meant we had certain privileges, and being a captain of the track team and co-captain of the football team gained me respect, but you had to be careful about who you went out with. If you were with a white girl the police would stop you and question you about it.

There's a lot made about athletics being the great equalizer; that once you put on a football uniform and go out on the field, nobody really cares what color you are. That's true. It's a team effort, a team sport. As football players we depended upon each other to do the job, and all through high school, after I'd established that I was the star on the team and they needed me, they accepted me. But I was so naive that I thought that meant I was accepted in general. A week after graduation I went downtown one day to the bowling alley. It's all white.

When I walk in the door there's one of our track stars, and he looks at me and says, "What are you doing in here? We don't allow no niggers in here." We'd been on the track team together! When he said that, we went to it. I knocked him down and we had a fight, and the police were called and they took me off. So there's a condition: people accept you for what they need from you.

By the time they divorced a couple of years later my mother and my stepfather had been together almost twenty years, and all of that time I never said more than good morning or good afternoon to him. We just did not get along. I respected him, but we didn't lose any time talking to one another. Sometimes he'd put his arm around me and say, "Son," you know, but that was it. It was just my mother and me, and she shielded me from him, made sure that he didn't put a hand on me. When they got divorced it was nothing to me. We had a little hard time, but then the war started and my mother got hired by the Chrysler Motor Corporation and started working in their factory. She had a little numbers route, too, helping me out. By that time I was in dental school. I figured soon I would be in the army or practicing dentistry and I could take care of her.

4

This Type of Problem...

I GRADUATED FROM high school in 1936, a year before my stepfather got busted for running numbers. In the spring of '36, after a track meet at Ann Arbor, I began writing my application to the University of Michigan. I wanted all the words to be spelled right and all the punctuation to be right, so it took me a couple of days, and I just had it done when these recruiters from the University of Detroit came to my house. Larry Bleach was a basketball player, an outstanding All American who was the only black student at the University of Detroit at that time. He and an assistant coach had come to recruit me to play football and run track. They talked to me: "Hey, we'll give you a free ride; we'll buy your books . . . ."

I said, "Well, this sounds pretty good. I'll come out to look at your school." But first I took my application up to Ann Arbor, to the University of Michigan, and turned it in. It was accepted and I was admitted to Michigan on a football scholarship. They were allowed to have just one black player on the football team at a time, and Willis Ward was a senior, and he was graduating, so I would have been the next; but I only stayed two weeks. They had Tommy Harmon there and Forest Evaschevski, and Tommy Harmon and all the white football players stayed in the frat houses; but fraternities wouldn't accept blacks, and blacks couldn't stay in a dormitory at the University of Michigan, so they were going to put me in a room in the gymnasium. They wanted me to live in the gym! The coach told me, "Our black player either has to stay here in the gym or room in the city with a black family." But I figured that at the University of Detroit I could live at home and go back and forth to school, so I left Ann Arbor, went home and enrolled at Detroit. There my athletic scholarship paid for my books, tuition and all that stuff, and I was given a job on campus. They called it the NYA, the National Youth Administration—some type of federal program that gave me spending money. And in the summer the university got jobs for us at Ford Motor Company; all the athletes would work in a group at Ford.

The University of Detroit was a Jesuit university, a Catholic university like Villanova, Duquesne, Boston College, Santa Clara, Notre Dame. We had to sit out our freshman year—we could only play three years of college athletics at that time—but although we couldn't play in games, our freshman team scrimmaged against the varsity. The priests would watch us practice. In one of our scrimmages a Hispanic guy out of New York was the varsity quarterback. I ran him down and tackled him for a loss two or three times, and he got angry about it. He

got up and screamed, "You black son of a bitch . . . . "
He didn't have time to finish what he was going to say,
because I was on him. We fought right there on the field.
As we fought I was using pretty foul language, and a
priest separated us and said, "Now, stop this!" So I went
into the dressing room. I took off my shoulder pads so I
could swing; took off my football shoes and put on my
tennis shoes so I wouldn't slip, because I knew that when
the quarterback came in we were going to continue the
fight. But he walks through the door and says,
"McMillan, I didn't mean to call you those names. No
hard feelings." I said, "OK. I just want you to remember
that every time you do that we're going to mix it up.
We're going to have at it." You had to protect your turf.

I had other problems that first semester. George
Jackson and I got in trouble with our grades and for
dating the wrong girls. I began paying less attention to
the ladies and more attention to my studies, but raising
my grades wasn't easy. They were low because I hadn't
learned the college system yet. It was simple: you have to
conserve your time. But I was taking Chemistry and
English, and I was carrying eighteen credits and practicing football. To be in college with all this glamorous
stuff around you, it's tough if you don't arrange your
time right. And I hadn't. I got a couple of Cs and a
couple of Ds and an F and eventually they kicked me off
the team; but they gave me the next semester to make up
my grades. I made them up and then I could play the
following year, but George Jackson left and went to
Morehouse College, where he competed in athletics.

I think I was the second Afro-American to enroll in the University of Detroit and be in the athletic program. I know I was the only Afro-American playing on the football team, but I had a camaraderie with my team-mates and the other students in my classes. There wasn't any real social prejudice that you could see—I would go across the street with my friends to the bars and to the German Club and what have you. Prejudice came to the surface in another form.

As a sophomore I was a starter on the football team. We played southern football teams, and the university wouldn't let me go into the South with the team. Afro-Americans in Oklahoma and North Carolina and Texas clipped news stories out of their local newspapers and sent them to me. The week before a game with us on their turf, it would be in all the papers that the University of Detroit had a negro on its team and he would not be allowed to play in the game. I kept the clippings and thought about what they meant. Even when southern teams came to Detroit, the coaches had second thoughts about letting me in; but our newspapers played it up so, and there was so much controversy about it that they relented. I played against southern teams at our stadium.

The first time something happened was when we played against Purdue down in Indiana. Hell, Indiana isn't even in the South, but Indiana is southern racist; it's not just the states of the Old Confederacy. When we got to the South Bend hotel where the team was staying, its manager didn't want me there. The coach came to me and said, "You can't stay in the hotel. We're going to let you stay across town with a nice colored family."

At the University of Detroit, 1937: "I was the only Afro-American on the football team."

"Well, Coach, I'm not going to do that. Either I stay in the hotel with the team and play in the game or you can send me home."

So they talked and they negotiated with the hotel owner, and some of my teammates gathered around me and we discussed it, and they let me stay in the hotel. I played against Purdue, but the coach wouldn't take me with the team on southern trips from then on because he knew that they'd have this type of problem. But I didn't let it bother me, and in 1938 I made Honorable Mention on the Catholic All-American Football Team.

My junior year I was openly going with a caucasian girl. We spent time together on the campus. I was on the practice field one afternoon during the spring term when the dean of the college of Arts & Science, a Jesuit priest, called me into his office. I got dressed and went in and sat down. He said, "Well, McMillan, your grades don't suggest that you are really a college level student. You'll have difficulty in life if you don't do better, so I'm not going to let you play football your senior year." That was a shock! I was just a slightly below average student playing football and track and trying to get an education. And I was a liberal arts major, but my grades were as good as some of these other kids that were playing right next to me who were majoring in commerce or physical education or what have you. I felt that the dean and the college were discriminating against me because I was black. I said, "Well, I appreciate your being interested in my education, but I want to play. Next year is my last year, and I believe I can make All American." The dean said, "That may be, but I can not condone you walking around the campus holding hands with Mary ___."

Mary ___ was a stunning young lady with long red hair. We were just good friends (maybe because I was a football star), but it looked like we were really going together when we were seen on the campus under the trees, talking and holding hands and spending time together. I wanted it to be something more than friendship, but it wasn't—it just looked bad. When it got back to Mary's family, who were big donors to the university and very prominent people in the Detroit area, they called Father Quinn. He said, "This will stop!"

I said, "Father Quinn, you mean to tell me that you're going to put me out of school?" I said, "You're a priest sitting behind that desk with that collar turned around, and I'm a Catholic, and you make that statement to me?"

He said, "Look, McMillan, I know you. You're pretty foxy, but you're not going to make me feel bad about it. You asked, and that's what it is."

Remember what Lincoln Continentals used to look like when they first came out? The first model was a phaeton—it looked like a convertible, and the top would come back. Mary had a Continental. She would come to my house and pick me up in this open convertible, and we'd go for a ride and the police would stop us. When she showed them her driver's license they knew who she was, how important she was, and they'd let us go. The university just did not want this to happen. I've never seen Mary ___ since.

5

"Remember This"

I WAS KICKED OFF the football and track teams and stripped of my athletic scholarship. I stayed in school, but I had to start paying my own way, so I started working at the Ford Motor Company from four o'clock until midnight, going to classes in the daytime. Back then you could go to college for two years and two summers and get enough credits to be accepted in a medical or dental school; you didn't have to have a bachelor's degree. I decided to try to get into a dental school, and I took biochemistry and biology and other courses to make up for deficiencies and raise some of the grades that I had that were below par. It took me a couple of years more at the University of Detroit to get prepared, but I succeeded.

I had been partially inspired to go into dentistry by the example of Dr. Haley Bell, a black dentist in Hamtramck. He had a nice office and he was a big show guy—big ring and big cars—and he had all the white practice. He was known in Hamtramck; he was very important. There were a couple of other black physicians in the community. One was an OB-GYN guy who got involved in abortions. He made plenty of money. The other physician was Dr. Houston, who worked for the city. He was a decent, honest physician, and a good man.

Dr. Bell was not only a successful dentist, he was also the bag man for the mayor of Hamtramck; the numbers people would bring the money to him in his office. Say a runner picked up a thousand dollars on his route—the runner's thing was 10 percent of that, and he turned over the rest of it to the house, to the guys who were backing the game. These guys, the Mafia or the underworld people, had to pay off the mayor, so they would give that part of it to Haley Bell, and he would take it to the mayor. Eventually everybody got caught, but my mother saved Dr. Bell from going to jail with her political connections. She went to the prosecuting attorney and told him, "This man is important in the black community. You can't send him to jail. I worked for you and got you elected with the black vote, and I need this favor from you." They set him free.

In their medical practices the black physicians and the dentist were inspirations to me. I had also learned something about life from the Dutchman who owned the house we had lived in in the ghetto. He taught me how to do plumbing and he taught me about finances and the work ethic as well: When we first moved to the ghetto, we couldn't even afford to pay rent. This Dutchman owned ten or twelve houses. One of them was vacant and in disrepair, and to keep it from being torn apart by poor people who wanted the wood for their cooking fires and heat et cetera, he was astute enough to let us live in it. We agreed to dig a basement under it for him and paint the house and do these things to live there for free until my dad got a job and we could pay rent. There was a vacant lot next to that house on Denton Street, and a factory was behind it. As we were digging the basement we put the dirt out on this vacant lot and smoothed it around and didn't think anything of it. Then the factory started hiring people, and they were looking for parking spaces. I didn't know whose lot it was, but I started parking cars on it and charging people fifty cents a week. I'd been doing this for three months when one day I went out to collect the money and the people told me, "We don't have to pay you any more. This is not your lot. We paid the Dutchman. He owns this property." I ran into the house and told my mother. She didn't say anything.

The Dutchman came that afternoon and I jumped on him. I said, "Why did you ruin me? Why did you take my business and take all my money?" The Dutchman was always talking to me about how I should work and be industrious and go to school and study; he would tell me about his houses and how he was living well in the Depression. But he said, "Look, let me tell you one thing, young man. You must realize that you can't take people's property. This is my lot. You didn't come to me and ask to rent it so you could make some money, so I just kicked you off of it and I'm taking all the money. Remember this." I did.

6

Not a Communist

BEFORE WORLD WAR II the Communists were going around giving picnics for the black people and inviting them to these picnics, telling them they were going to have white girls out there so that these black men could go with them. We'd go out to the picnics and eat their food and bullshit with them, and they wanted to sign us up for the Communist party against the United States. And the Germans had rallies in Madison Square Garden talking about the destruction of the United States, and the Italians and the Japanese had their secret service people going throughout the United States in black communities trying to recruit us to turn against our country. I went to all of the picnics, the commie picnics, the German picnics, the Japanese picnics—food, ice cream . . . you know. And the United States was letting this crap go on.

At that time my mother took in a black man that was down and out, and we fed him and gave him a little money and he did a lot of things for us. Elijah Muhammad was just getting the Black Muslims started in Detroit. They recruited this man who lived with us, and he finally joined them. They changed him 100 percent— he started washing his face, shaving, working. They gave him a push cart and he was collecting papers and stuff. The Muslims had a warehouse in the middle of our street, and this guy worked there every day for a while, but he finally drifted away from the organization. One day, long before Pearl Harbor, I ran into this guy, and we were standing there on the street talking when a Ford Trimotor airplane flew over. The guy fell down on his knees and said, "Oh, please don't bomb us." He thought that the plane was Japanese. I went on my way, but it stayed in my mind that the Japanese were in the United States recruiting blacks to overthrow this country, telling them what was happening and what was going to happen.

In the summer of 1942 I was working at the Ford factory to earn money to pay for my fall tuition. At Ford I was a committeeman for the UAW in the foundry. I kept track of all the union people to make sure that the company followed the contracts, to make sure that everybody was getting the right amount of money. While doing this and working with black people I kept talking about the segregated military—"Blacks can't fight and die for our country in combat like every other citizen. Instead they segregate us in service units, make us truck drivers and so forth. I say it's a shame, and I'm not going to war if I can't be an infantryman or run a tank or fly an airplane. If I've got to drive a truck or handle garbage or something, I'm not going to go."

"Well, you pledge allegiance to the flag, don't you?"

"Hell no! I'm not going to stand and pledge allegiance. Why should I pledge allegiance to a god-damned country that doesn't even want me to go to war and die for it?" It was known throughout the factory what type of hot head I was, I guess. The foremen knew it, and I talked to everybody.

Ford had developed a way to make magnesium out of magnesium oxide. They built six big furnaces with retorts that ran through big round tubes to a gas furnace. We loaded these things with magnesium oxide, closed them up and put the vacuum on them so that they were in vacuum atmosphere, and heated them until the magnesium came out of the oxide. Then we drew it to the end of the tube and cut it off and took it out, and we had solid magnesium. I had two responsibilities: I had to read the pyrometer to make sure that the gas temperature was right, and I had to make sure that all the men on these six furnaces did the job that they were supposed to do. They had all black guys on this. This was skilled work, and they were making high wages.

This operation had been in the glass plant, it's where they had started it, and one day a bunch of white guys from the glass plant came over, and the foreman took my men off the furnaces and put the white guys on. My men were put to doing low-paid manual labor. The white guys were union people too, and I said, "What are you guys doing over here?"

"Well, they came over and got us from the glass plant and told us to come over here and work on these furnaces."

I said, "You know you are violating the union contract. Now get off of this job and go back to what you were doing or I'm going to see that you get put out of the goddamned union!" I said, "These black guys been here a long time and they should have the shelter of seniority." So the guys said, "OK, OK. We'll go." They walked off the furnaces and went back to the glass plant.

So now here's the foreman. The black guys are still doing the manual labor job they've been assigned, and the furnaces are unattended. The foreman says, "You made those white guys leave the furnaces; now put these black guys back to work on them."

I said, "I can't put anybody back to work. I'm a committeeman and I'm taking care of union business and doing my job. If you want somebody on those furnaces, you put them on. I don't give a shit if they burn up or not."

He said, "Well, I'm not going to." He wouldn't put anybody back on the furnaces, and they burned up. He finally went around and cut off the gas (they were gas fired), but it was too late. All those retorts, tubes . . . just melted up!

Harry Bennett came out. Bennett was head of security at Ford, and he had tried to take over the company when old man Ford got senile. He brought his security people and army people in uniforms, and they all came out and saw these burned up furnaces. So the FBI and Harry Bennett took me back to the big Ford office complex and accused me of sabotage and of being a communist. They kept interrogating me and accusing me, and I kept saying, "I'm not a communist. I want to volunteer to go into the army. Hey, I'll go in the army tomorrow if you'll put me in the infantry or in the Army Air Corps. I want to *fight* for my country. I think this is the greatest country in the world. And I'm a Catholic, and you've never seen Catholics that are Communists. Look at my history and you'll see I went to a Catholic school." So they let it go. They didn't have a case against me anyway.

7

FDR

I HAD BEGUN TO DEVELOP some interest in politics when I was still pretty young. Before we moved to Michigan we had an old crystal radio set, and I remember sitting with my mother and stepfather in our living room listening to the results of the national elections of 1928 when Al Smith ran against Herbert Hoover. They were talking about Smith being a Democrat and what a nice guy he was—that his election would help black people and poor people. By the time Franklin Roosevelt ran for president in 1932 I was a dyed-in-the wool Democrat. I didn't know that in the South any number of blacks were Republicans. When I found out, it was really an enigma to me; but Lincoln freed the slaves and he was a Republican—why shouldn't black people be Republicans?

My mother was very active in politics when we lived in the ghetto down on Denton Avenue, and when I was in the sixth, seventh, and eighth grades she would hold political meetings at our home. I would hear her talk about how this councilman was going to run, and who was going to run for mayor of Hamtramck. I knew all of these people by name because I would go with my mother to some of the meetings or they would have them at our house. Political patronage was important to us: it got my mother a job as a clerk in the welfare department, and we would get favors down in the city, and politicians respected her. I knew that.

I lost money when the banks closed. I'd played a policy number and won, and I wanted to buy a bicycle; never had a bicycle in my life. My mother had bought me a pair of roller skates, and that was the only thing that I had to get around on, but she said, "Don't buy a bicycle with this money. Put it in the bank and start a savings account."

I said, "Oh Mom, no. I don't want to do that; I want a bicycle."

And she said, "No, we're going to start life out right for you; we're going to deposit this money in the bank."

After we had this big discussion I went up to the bank with her and we deposited the money, and a week later the banks folded. I said, "Can I get my money out of the bank?" She said no, and I said, "You see—you made me lose my money." When FDR opened the banks and started bank insurance, I thought he was the savior of the country. And Social Security and all of the other things that the Democratic Party did: the New Deal made me a solid Democrat for the rest of my life.

Before the CIO came in and started the United Auto Workers, when blacks went to work at the Ford Motor Company we didn't have a steady job. We were hired in August when the new model was started, and we worked until that model was finished, and then they laid us off until it was time to build the next year's cars. Now we didn't have any money coming in. If you hadn't saved while you were working, you would starve. You didn't get vacations and you didn't have any health insurance and you didn't have a steady job, but you would go back to the plant in the fall and go through the employment line and hope and pray that you would get your job back. There was no middle class—there were just rich people and the rest of society. The unions, in my opinion, are the only reason that we got a white middle class— they made middle class America. I was very active in the autoworkers union, and when we struck I was locked into the Ford plant and had fights outside and that type of thing. But Henry Ford gave in to the unions and gave us raises and 100 percent union membership—the company would deduct our dues from our wages and turn them over to the union, so everybody belonged. Roosevelt and the Democrats stood for the ordinary, common working guy, and they supported organized labor, respected the unions.

I began to lose my fascination with FDR when the war started. The military was still segregated and he was doing nothing about it. The army had segregated black units, and the NAACP and politicians and others were saying, "Hey, Roosevelt could change this if he wanted to." But he didn't, you know. So I lost respect for him . . .

kept it for his wife and the Democratic Party. But after the war the Dixiecrats out of the South were all Democrats and they controlled Congress and they weren't decent to black people, and I just didn't understand that; I was messed up in that.

8

"Mac, Don't Start Any Trouble"

MY DRAFT NUMBER came up in January of 1941. I was still at the University of Detroit, and I was also working at the Ford factory. When I flunked my physical (for a condition I prefer not to go into), they gave me a few months to get my health back. I finally went in as a second lieutenant in the army reserve because I was still in school and had almost three years of college . . . stayed in civilian clothes; you didn't have to put a uniform on. That year a big civil rights thing happened: A. Philip Randolph, head of the Pullman Porters Union, threatened to march on Washington to get equal employment rights for blacks, and he forced the government into taking some action.[*] There was a lot of discussion of this among my friends.

In the fall of 1941 I was admitted to the Meharry School of Dentistry in Nashville, Tennessee. I was still in the reserves, but after Pearl Harbor we were all to go into ASTC, the Army Specialized Training Corps—the military would pay for our books and tuition and everything, and we would go into the army as dentists when we graduated. At first I couldn't get into the ASTC, but all the other students at Meharry were accepted. They passed the physical examination; I didn't. To earn enough money to return to school in the fall, I worked at Ford again in the summer of 1942. Later I did pass the physical and finished my dental studies in the ASTC program.

While I was at Meharry I kept close to the civil rights movement as far as conversations went, but I wasn't active except when something pertained directly to me. There was always talk about the NAACP trying to make things better and about the need to fight the Ku Klux Klan, which was rampant throughout the South, and other stuff . . . but I was too involved in trying to stay in school and do my thing.

My last year in dental school I got married to Doleeta Moore, a student at Fisk University, right across the

---

[*]In the spring of 1941 trade unionist and civil rights leader A. Philip Randolph threatened to lead thousands of blacks in a march on Washington to protest employment discrimination in defense industries and federal bureaus. Shortly thereafter President Roosevelt issued an executive order barring such discrimination and creating the Fair Employment Practices Committee (FEPC). Randolph called off the march, but the FEPC proved to be relatively ineffective.

street from Meharry. Doleeta had been adopted. Her stepfather was a physician in Oklahoma City, had an Afro-American hospital there. Her mother was part black and part Indian, but her natural father was caucasian, and she looked as if she were a caucasian girl. Nashville was a segregated city, but Doleeta was so light she could go downtown to the theater by herself and sit downstairs, whereas the Afro-Americans had to sit up in the balcony. We started going together, and in March of my senior year we got married.

I graduated from dental school in 1944. They had accelerated our studies—we went all year round for the last two years, so that we finished in three rather than four years. After graduation we were given another physical exam before being commissioned lieutenants in the Army Dental Corps. I flunked again. This time the guy said, "You've got flat feet, and you can't lift your arm above your head. You're a limited service man. We're not taking limited service people in the army at this time." So I'm out of the army again.

I'm a dentist now, and I beat it back to Detroit where I get an interim license to practice from my dentist friend, Dr. Bell. (This will let me practice until the board exam is offered again.) I order my equipment from the dental supply house and go out to Inkster, where the big airport is now in Detroit. Rent a place and get ready to practice dentistry—figure there's a shortage of dentists and I can make a fortune before this war is over. I spend the day trying to get the place together and waiting for the guy to deliver my equipment (he never did), and when I get back home my mother says, "You got this letter." It was an "immediate action" letter from the

United States Army in an envelope with a big red border around it. It said I was to report to Carlisle Barracks in Pennsylvania within twenty-four hours under punishment of being court martialled. I was back in the army: apparently they had decided that they could use a dentist with flat feet and a bad shoulder. I told my wife, "I've got to go," and I caught the train and reported to Carlisle Barracks.

The town of Carlisle was still segregated. Here's how bad things were: they had German prisoners of war working on the base, and they could date American girls; they had free run of the base; they could go into town and go to the theater and sit in the first floor seats where the white people sat, and all black people who came into the theater had to sit in the balcony. It was obvious that blacks were unwelcome in Carlisle, so we'd catch the bus and go into Harrisburg to the black community, and find girls and fellows that we could associate with. Going back to base one night I get on the bus, and after about half an hour we stop to change drivers. (This was an army bus; they hired civilians to drive them.) I'm sitting in a front seat, and the new driver gets on the bus and looks at me and says, "Boy, you can't sit up here. You got to get in the back."

I'm a first lieutenant on my way overseas to fight for this country. I said, "You must be out of your cotton-picking mind."

He didn't start the bus. He said, "I'm not going to move this bus until you sit in the back."

"No way!"

He said, "If you don't sit in the back, I'm going to throw you off the bus."

Carlisle Barracks, Pa., 1945: "I was back in the army. Apparently they had decided they could use a dentist with flat feet and a bad shoulder."

I said, "Yeah? Try it!" So he got up to throw me off, and I put my foot in his stomach and pushed him out the door. Then I jumped out and let him have it.

The police came and took me to the base and turned me over to the MPs. I stayed in a cell overnight, and the next morning they took me to the general's office. He said, "Lieutenant, I'm surprised at you. You have to be an officer and a gentleman. What were you doing fighting and hitting an employee of the base?"

I said, "Sir, not with any disrespect, but I'll fight and kick him again. He had the nerve to tell me that I'd have to sit in the back of that bus, and he called me a nigger. It's a good thing that I didn't kill him, sir."

"What?"

"Yes sir, that's what happened."

The general said, "Release this man." And that afternoon he called the whole camp to attention, turned them out. He said, "I've learned of an incident that I will not put up with at this base. As long as I'm in command here, this type of thing will not happen. There will be no difference between races. We're all American soldiers and we're doing a job for our country and we're going to do it together. And by God, if you are on this base you'll respect every person as a human being." And he dismissed us.

After six weeks training at Carlisle Barracks I was assigned to Ft. Huachuca, Arizona. I decided to take my wife to her home in Oklahoma City before reporting for duty. The trip turned ugly when we got into the South.

Doleeta had lived in the black community in Oklahoma City, but her family was real prominent, and growing up she had had things her way, really—her stepfather was associated with some of the white physicians there, and she had free run of the city; and she was so light skinned that outside of Oklahoma City she could go anywhere she wanted to go, because people didn't know whether she was black or white. Since Doleeta wasn't accustomed to rigid segregation, we had difficulty traveling together. She would get me into trouble by running her mouth. I would say, "You know, you've got to realize what you're saying." We got as far as Chicago all right, but from Chicago to Oklahoma City the train was segregated. We had to change trains in Memphis, and while we were waiting we decided to leave the station and walk around a little. A policeman drove up to the curb and said, "Come here, boy!"

I was the only *man* on the sidewalk, but I walked over to the car and said, "Yes?"

"What are you doing with that white woman?"

"That happens to be my wife, sir, and she's not white."

He looked her over and he said, "Well, she damn sure looks white." Then he says, "Well, I know that you're not from Memphis, because around here no niggers get up this early in the morning. You either have to be a preacher or an undertaker, and . . . . What *are* you doing out on the street at this time of night, nigger?"

"Oh, we're waiting for the train to Oklahoma City."

"OK, you go back in that station, back in there where the niggers stay, and don't you come out until you get your train."

I said, "Yes, sir."

When it came time to board we were a little late getting to the platform, so we started running to get on before the train left the station. My wife was ahead of me, and the conductor reached out his hand and helped her on the train. I'm right behind her and I get ready to step up and he says, "No, nigger, you go to the next car." Doleeta says, "That's my husband!" So he pushes her off the train too, and we have to run up to the next car to get on.

Stuff like that happened all the time. It hadn't been too bad in Detroit, but in the South it was awful. Military police would come up and harass you and want to know what you were doing with that white woman and that type of thing, and you had to put up with it because you didn't know when they were going to hit you over the head with a stick or lock you up.

Ft. Huachuca, Arizona, was where the 7th Cavalry had been stationed, and the 10th cavalry, the Buffalo Soldiers, the black soldiers. That's where the army formed up to fight Pancho Villa and the Mexicans. Pershing had his black cavalry there. During World War II all black soldiers were sent to that base—the 92nd and 93rd divisions and all the medical personnel, hospital people . . . that's where they sent us to stage us before they shipped us out to different places. We were being formed into hospital type units—from there you would either be assigned to a battalion or you would to go a hospital or you'd go to a dental clinic somewhere.

We had fifteen to eighteen thousand black soldiers in Ft. Huachuca at times (first time in my life I'd ever seen a black colonel), and there may have been three hundred white soldiers. On the base was a white hospital and a black hospital. The black hospital had black physicians and dentists and staff, and the white hospital had whites. Black physicians and dentists couldn't work on white soldiers or white families anywhere in the army then; they could only work on black people. But white doctors could work on both races, and a white major was head of our dental clinic, which had all black dentists. The two hospitals must have been five miles or more outside the main gate of Ft. Huachuca in a little town called Nogales. Some town . . . but they had a big beer garden, and the soldiers would go there and girls would come and dance. (A white general stationed at the fort owned that bar.) We also had an officers club where things could get pretty wild.

Four of my classmates from Meharry were at Ft. Huachuca with me, and we just raised hell. We'd go to Mexico, buy rum and put it in the cooler and have parties. These older black soldiers, majors and captains and what have you, had their wives there, and we'd go to the officer's club and dance with their wives and raise all kinds of hell. One night when I was having a particularly good time the colonel sent somebody over to my table to take me to him. "You are a disgrace to the United States Army Officers Corps," he said. "You're supposed to be a soldier and a gentleman, but here you are drunk and cavorting and carrying on. I'm going to see to it that you get shipped out of here, shipped so far around the world from the United States that if you take one more step you'll be back in this country!"

Two days later I got orders for Calcutta, India; so did my classmates. But first we had to go through some additional training at Camp Shanks, New York. I was to be the officer in charge of 126 black soldiers, enlisted personnel who were going to India with us, plus eleven other black officers that were with me. So I was the commanding officer, and this kind of detached me. These enlisted men had been in an army jail for three years in North Carolina where all they had done was march and work, I guess. These guys could march! So I took them and the officers who were assigned to me to Boston to board a ship and go overseas. There were also 135 American Red Cross women on the ship. They were treated as officers, and four or five of them were black.

The enlisted soldiers were kept down in the hot, smelly hold of that ship, puking and vomiting while the Red Cross women and us officers were all upstairs where it was cool and we could breathe fresh air. These kids wanted to mutiny. They wanted to break out, but marines travel on these ships to enforce law and order, and the marines had their guns on them and were going to shoot. The army commander of the troops on the ship called me and said, "I want you to go downstairs and see if you can keep these men from rioting. If you don't, they're going to get killed."

I said, "You're going to send me down in there after you're treating these people this bad? They'll kill me. If I'm going down there by myself to talk to them about being nice, you've got to change the rules and regulations. You've got to let these soldiers come up on the deck for air during the day, and feed them and treat them decently. If I get that kind of commitment from you I'll go; if not, I won't."

He said OK, so I went down and these guys said, "Oh, you think you're a big shot coming down here?" And I said, "Wait a minute fellows. Listen to me." I went on and told them what the offer was, and they finally accepted it.

When we were in the Mediterranean the weather was nice and the girls would come up and put on their shorts and sun bathe. They would come out and sit all over the deck, forcing us twelve black officers to stand around the sides; there was no place for us to sit. After dinner one night I said, "We're going to stop this bullshit. We're going to get out there first and we're going to get in the middle of that damned deck and let's see what happens."

The guys said, "Oh, no. You're going to get us put in the brig."

I said, "Well, if you guys won't, I will."

The next morning I got up and went out and sat right in the middle of the place. There was nobody else on the deck. Shortly the girls started coming out and they would sit at the edges, around and away from me, this black speck sitting out there in the middle. Finally, when there was no other place left, the late arrivals began sitting near me. Up on top I could see the army commander and the commanding officer of the Red Cross women, and they looked madder than hell. The next day I did this again, and the colonel called me into his office. He had the Red Cross commanding officer there, and he said, "Lieutenant, we don't like what we see out there. You're sitting amongst all these Red Cross women who are scarcely clothed, and you're looking around at them, and we don't want you to sit out there any more."

I said, "You mean to tell me that I can't sit on the deck, sir?"

"No, you can't sit on the deck amongst all these white women."

I said, "Well, I guess the only other place you have for me is in the brig, because every day I'm going to come sit down." He let it go, and then the other black officers came out and sat on the deck and they started talking to the girls. He couldn't do anything about it, I guess; he could, but he didn't want to. So everything went well from there until we landed at Calcutta.

We got assigned to Kanchurpura, which was about sixty miles east of Calcutta. The 49th Ordnance Battalion and a general hospital were on that base. The 49th was a battalion of black soldiers with no black officers—the highest ranking black man in the outfit was a master sergeant. They stored all of the ammunition for the navy, the army and what have you. Our group of replacements included a black ordnance officer for the 49th, a black provost marshal (military police), and us two dentists. The black military policeman was put out in the field to be head of all the security, and he replaced a white captain who commanded the detachment of Gurkha Rifles that was guarding the post. The Gurkhas were Nepalis and they were tremendous fighters—they carried these damn bull knives and they'd cut your head off in a minute—but they wouldn't give our military police guy any respect.

Before we arrived, the dental clinic at Kanchurpura was staffed with two Jewish officers and four white enlisted men, and the medical clinic was staffed with a white medical officer and four white enlisted men. So two black dentists took over the dental clinic. Our job was to do the simple things—fillings, extractions, cleanings, that type of thing. We hadn't had any postgraduate work at that time, so if there were any real difficult problems we would take our patients over to the general hospital where they had only white officers. These white dentists had been practicing for years in the army, and they had the plush jobs and they did the surgery and a lot of the other things. Surgery was the biggest thing.

The white officer who ran the medical clinic was our commanding officer. When we reported he sent the two of us down to live at the dental clinic instead of putting us in the bachelor officers quarters. I looked over where we were going to stay, and I said, "Man, I tell you, this is bad and getting worse. We're going to stay in the BOQ or else."

My friend said, "Mac, don't start any trouble."

I said, "Hell, I'm not going to stay down here." Really, that was the best place to stay because you were close to the work, but I said, "Nope. I think they're being unfair to us."

We went down to the mess hall and they didn't have us segregated there at all. We sat at a table with a southern second lieutenant, two captains (one from Harvard and one from Yale), and there was another white guy from New York. When we sat down, this southern officer (he was from Florida; had been some kind of a judge back there), he got up and moved and sat at the next table. Things went along OK for a while, and then all of a sudden he started up and you could hear his voice all over the damn mess. He was going on about what dirty people niggers were, and how he treated them in his court; talking about how the police would drag them in drunk, and he'd sentence them, and they'd be thrown in a cell, kicked around. No respect for any of us.

I told the two captains at my table, "Fellows, I'm tired of this. This has to come to a stop."

One said, "Mac, don't get yourself in any trouble. He's not worth it."

I said, "It's worth it to me. I'm a first lieutenant in the United States Army, and I think I should have the respect of that position. If that fellow don't like me, at least he should respect the uniform."

"What are you going to do?"

"I'm going over there and shut his mouth."

He said, "You'll get in trouble if you hit him. You're his superior, you know; you're a first lieutenant and he's a second."

"I don't care. I'm going to go over there and stop him." So I got up from the table and went over there and told him, "I'm tired of your conversation about negroes, or 'niggers' as you say. I don't want to hear it any more." And I pushed up to him and got right in his face and egged him on, and he was angry and upset and he drew back and hit me. That's what I wanted him to do—hit me so I could shut him up for good.

The major from the outfit called me in to his office the next morning: "I understand you had a fight in the mess hall last night."

"Yes sir, I had a fight. Your lieutenant hit me. I figured I had a right to protect myself, and I knocked him down and that stopped him."

"He hit you first?"

"Yes, he did."

He said, "You're smart enough to incite that, aren't you?"

"Not me, sir. I don't know that much about army law. I'm a dentist working in the army, and I don't know all this other stuff."

So he said, "Well, I know you're a little smarter than that. I understand that you want me to move you into the BOQ. You don't want to stay in the dental clinic; you thought that we put you there to segregate you. You're wrong. All of the white officers who served in your position stayed down there too. We thought that this was more convenient, and that's why I decided to put you guys there. Now we're going to move you up into the barracks. Be careful. Don't get into any more trouble."

I said, "OK. Thank you sir, but I want you to tell certain people to respect officers, to watch their mouths."

He said, "I will," and that ended all the problems.

India blew my mind. The caste system existed there, and Anglo-Indian people in Calcutta had all the plush jobs. They worked in the post office; they worked in offices with telephones and all that, and dark Indians had the filthy, dirty jobs. I couldn't understand why the American army would segregate its own people in a black country. The first time we went into Calcutta on a pass we discovered that the American Red Cross had tents in two places about a mile apart. They had black girls working in an American Red Cross tent for blacks, and white girls working in a separate one for whites. Signs in front of the tent for whites read, "No niggers or dogs allowed."

I was there about a year and we had only one accident on the base. A company of black soldiers was on its last detail; they were scheduled to go home the following day. They were taking ten trunks of Chinese gun powder out to destroy it—put it in a revetment and throw a grenade into it. These fellows were all riding in the back of the truck, and some guy that didn't know what he was doing was fooling around and he hit one of those cans of gun powder with a pick and ignited it and killed them all instantly. That was the first time I had seen a mushroom cloud like an atomic bomb; that's the way this thing went up. The army assigned all black soldiers to that type of duty—driving trucks, laboring, moving loads . . . service. That was what their job was until Patton took the 25th Regiment into the Battle of the Bulge, where he used them as soldiers.

I got promoted to captain while I was there. They brought a black medical officer down and made him commanding officer of our place, and I told him, "Hey, I'd like you to put me in for captain," and he did and I got promoted. Shortly after that they began moving troops out of India and into China to get ready to invade Japan. We were at a staging area getting ready to go, but after we had gotten our stuff together the orders for all the black units were changed. Some were to go to Korea, but most were being sent back to the States. The white units were still on for China, and the white officers couldn't understand it. Why did they have to get ready to invade Japan while blacks went back to the United States to get discharged? It puzzled me too.

I had some connections with the vice president of the American Red Cross in India, a caucasian woman that I had been complaining to about segregation. We were pretty good friends, and I told her, "You know, we'll be leaving India, but we're not going to China with everybody else. I don't know why, but our orders were changed and now we're going home." She said, "You haven't heard? I got it from a first class source that the orders for the negro soldiers were changed because Madame Chiang Kai-shek didn't want any blacks in China." And that was the truth. So we came back to the United States and all the white guys went up the Burma Road to China.

I had a lucky thing happen. My buddy and I had orders to board a plane to return to the States, but the night before we were to leave we went out and got plastered and overslept and missed our plane. That airplane crashed and killed all aboard somewhere in Turkey. So we got on another airplane, a C-54, and we went through Saigon, the Philippines, Guam . . . . Landed and went through customs in Hawaii, and then came on into San Francisco.

My orders directed me on to Chicago to get discharged. I told my buddy, "Hey, man, we don't have to catch the train until tomorrow morning; let's go to the officers club." We started up to the club, and just as we got to the door we ran into the general. He looked at us and said, "Where you boys going?"

We said, "We're going to the officers club."

"Don't you know we don't allow negroes in here?"

"Well, this is an officers club on an army base."

"Yeah," he said, "but this is the permanent club. We have that officers club there in that tent for you colored boys."

I said to my buddy, "Forget it. We're too close to getting out and getting back home to have more troubles." So we left and the next morning we caught our trains—I was going to Chicago and he got on a train going to Nashville, Tennessee. It took me about a week to get cleared out of Chicago and come on back home. My experiences with racism in the army had made me an angry young man, and I stayed angry for a long time.

9

A Fresh Start

M Y LOVE, MY DAUGHTER JERI, had been born while I was overseas, but when I returned Doleeta and I separated and thought about getting a divorce. I took the state board examinations to make sure that I could practice dentistry, and then I had to decide where I was going to practice. Housing was hard to find after the war, so I moved in with my mother in Hamtramck and started practicing there. Eventually my wife and I changed our minds and got together again, and she got pregnant with my son James, who was born in 1947. We'd been married for about four years when Doleeta decided that she was going to leave and take the two children. It was a very hard thing. She brought the two youngsters to my office and we had a discussion about the separation, and she got angry and walked out of the office and left them with me. We were living in an apartment in a project at that time. Housing was hard to get ahold of, and it was out in a little Afro-American community in Detroit, what we called Eight Mile Road.

Doleeta was actually a very fine person. We just disagreed. When we got divorced in 1949 she went to Washington, D.C., where she got into the entertainment business, working in night clubs as an exotic dancer. Since I spent every day at my office, I had to make arrangements to have the children taken care of. I rented a house for an elderly woman and paid her to take care of them. Paid for her food and stuff, and I lived in the basement while my youngsters had bedrooms upstairs.

Doctor Charles West was the person who discovered Las Vegas for me. He was a Dartmouth graduate, a medical doctor who helped me get started in my dental practice in Detroit after the war; we practiced right across the street from each other. His father was a professor of anatomy at Howard University, and his mother was superintendent of schools, and his sisters were all teachers. They were first class people back in Washington.

Dr. West was married to a young lady, but he got a divorce, and I got divorced. His brother had served in Africa in World War II . . . stayed there and was in business in Liberia—he had an ice cream factory and a grocery and had a little hospital going. We had nothing else to do and we wanted some adventure, so we decided to go to Africa to practice medicine and dentistry together; but before it could happen Dr. West met this woman from Los Angeles and married her. They used to drive back and forth to visit her family, and one year they ran into storms and had to come through Las

Vegas. Dr. West knew a lot of the entertainers, and he liked the night life, and his wife liked the night life, so he decided to move to Las Vegas. "It's in Nevada," he said. "They have gambling and the town stays open twenty-four hours a day. And all the entertainers . . . . " I said, "OK, I'm sorry to see you go. This means we won't be going to Africa."

One winter morning after Dr. West left I dug my car out of the ice and got to my office, and the heater was bad and people were tracking snow and mud into the waiting room, and it was just awful. Didn't do much for your frame of mind. Nothing else was going right in my life either, and I wanted out. When I got my mail there was a postcard from a friend in Phoenix, Arizona—it had a big orange on it and the sun was shining. My son had a chest type thing when he was two years old, and the doctor had said, "You need to move your son to Arizona if he's going to outgrow this thing." Well, I couldn't just leave and go to Arizona, but Dr. West was in Las Vegas practicing, and I knew he would help me get started there. I called him and said, "Doc, what's the temperature in Las Vegas?"

"It's seventy-five degrees."

"I'm coming out."

I went out for a visit, but I couldn't just make a permanent move. First I had to straighten out my affairs and get some money together. And I wanted to pass the Nevada boards before I relocated my family.

A couple of years after my divorce the Korean War started. As a captain in the reserves, I was called back into the army. I resisted going—I had these two youngsters to take care of, but the army said that wasn't its problem; that I must do something with the children and report to Camp McCoy in Wisconsin. We negotiated this back and forth for over two years. Finally I decided to go ahead and sell my practice and go back in the army.

I wanted to leave the children with my mother, but she was getting married again, and she said, "No, I'm not going to take care of them. You better make other arrangements." So I arranged for this elderly lady to continue taking care of them, and I negotiated with the army to send me to Fort Benjamin Harrison near Indianapolis so that I could go back and forth to kind of monitor them. By this time the war was over, and the day before I was supposed to leave I got a telegram from the medical corps in Chicago telling me I didn't have to go. But I had sold my practice and made all my arrangements, and I had my mind set; I just put that telegram in my pocket and ignored it. Very early the next morning I got in my automobile and drove down to Ft. Benjamin Harrison.

I got to the base at 7:30 a. m., showed the officer of the day my original orders, and signed in. He says "We don't open till eight o'clock. Come back then and we'll start processing." So I came back at eight o'clock and a captain was there. He says, "McMillan, you're not supposed to be here. Your orders were cancelled."

I said, "Nobody told me they were cancelled. I've got my orders here and I've signed the book. I'm in the army. That's what you guys wanted, so here I am."

The captain called Chicago, and this major that I had been negotiating with told him, "Put Captain McMillan on the phone." I got on the phone and he said,

"What in the hell are you doing there? I sent you a telegram cancelling your orders."

"I didn't get any telegram. Maybe it's somewhere, but I didn't get it. I assumed that I had to report for duty, and I came here and signed in."

He says, "Well, you got me in a pickle now."

"Tough," I said. "I'm in the army and I'll stay."

I just had to get the hell away from Detroit, change my life. Everything was going bad. The divorce . . . and I was running around boozing and chasing women—not the life that I should have. Also I was half way busted, didn't have much money, and selling the practice for the little I got hadn't helped. Going into the army would give me a chance to get straightened out. It was part of my plan for a brighter future: I'd save my army pay and use it to get a fresh start in Las Vegas.

While I was still in the army, I flew out to visit Dr. West. Leaving the Las Vegas airport I got a rude awakening. I got in a cab and told the driver I wanted to go to Wyatt Avenue. He says, "Wyatt Avenue; I don't know where that is." So he gets on his radio and calls the office. He says, "I got a passenger. I'm trying to find Wyatt Avenue. Can you tell me how to get there?" The dispatcher says, "Yes, that's in the Westside, over where the niggers live," and she gives him directions. He apologized for what she had said, and then we drove off. We got to the corner of "D" Street and Bonanza, which were unpaved. The dust was flying up from cars driving by, and people were hanging out there in the dust outside a bar. We drove on to Wyatt Avenue, which was paved.

The only medical care available to black citizens in Las Vegas at that time was in the county hospital. There wasn't a doctor's office on the Westside until Dr. West arrived. He had bought two houses on Wyatt Avenue, and he had an office in one. When I got there he was busy, so I sat in his waiting room for a while. It was just crowded with people. At the twelve o'clock break he had a call to go to the Moulin Rouge, and he said, "Come with me. I want to show you a place."* We went up to the Moulin Rouge to this fellow's room, and learned he had partied all night and had a big hangover. Doc examined him and gave him a shot to stop his headache. The guy says, "Hey, there are some chips on the dresser. Take your fee in chips." Dr. West went over to the dresser where there was a stack of chips several inches high. He picked up just four of them.

I said, "Is that it? Is that your fee?"

"Yes."

When we got out to the car I said, "Well, what are these things worth?"

"A hundred dollars apiece."

I said, "You mean to tell me you were paid four hundred dollars on this house call?"

"Yes."

I said, "This is the place for me!"

---

*The Moulin Rouge, at 900 Bonanza Road, was located within the predominantly black Westside neighborhood. When it opened in 1957 it was the first major hotel-casino in Las Vegas to be interracial. For a variety of reasons the Moulin Rouge came to occupy a central place in the history of civil rights in Las Vegas. See Earnest N. Bracey, "The Moulin Rouge Mystique," *Nevada Historical Society Quarterly*, 39:4 (Winter 1996), 272-288.

   While I was at Ft. Benjamin Harrison I started going
with a young woman who worked in the hospital in
Detroit, and we decided to get married. Her name was
Magnolia Rutherford, but I called her Micki. She was a
model, modeled clothes for *Ebony*—a beautiful woman
who looked like she was anything but Afro-American.
She was very light, had long hair down her back. We got
married in Las Vegas. I was taking thirty days leave from
the army, and we drove out and took out our marriage
license and got married in the Moulin Rouge. Sammy
Davis Jr. was there, Billy Eckstine . . .   Ed Sullivan
happened to be in the Moulin Rouge at that time, and
Billy Daniels sang the wedding song for us. These people
were just there for the entertainment. That was the only
integrated hotel in town at that time, and all of these
people . . . . Betty Hutton, the wealthy heiress, was there.
And when we had the wedding, all these people just
came out and had a party.
   At that time West Las Vegas was really growing. It
had the Louisiana Club, Town Tavern, El Rio . . . . All
of these places were doing good business, so some white
people from Los Angeles, one was in the restaurant
business, had built the Moulin Rouge to get in on the
action. It was the only integrated hotel in Las Vegas, a
tremendous hotel, and all types of people visited it. Afro-
American chorus girls came out of Atlantic City and New
York to perform there, and most of the prominent black
entertainers came to the Moulin Rouge to perform. Part
of its appeal was that the entertainment went on all night
long. The hotels on the Strip had only two shows, one at
about eight o'clock and the other at twelve. After the
second show there was nothing really doing on the Strip

except the gambling, so all of the cocktail waitresses, entertainers, pit boss people and so forth from the late shift would come to the Moulin Rouge and just have a ball from about two o'clock until dawn.

The Moulin Rouge was a tremendous success and an immediate asset for the West Las Vegas area. Too bad that the owners couldn't get along. When the hotel closed a few months later it wasn't because of not having any business; it closed because the partners just couldn't get along and they decided not to pay any more bills. It was rumored that each of them would go into the boxes and put money into their pockets at the end of the night, and finally they just closed down. They didn't want anything more to do with it because they couldn't trust one another.[*]

I had passed the Nevada board exams, but I didn't get my notification from the board for almost two and a half months. Then I finally received my state license, and after my discharge from the army we moved to Las Vegas. Dr. Quannah McCall was an Indian who was a dentist, and he was on the state board. (His daughter Connie is still practicing.) When I opened my office, he came to congratulate me and wish me well. We sat and talked for a while, and I asked him why it had taken so long for the board to award me my license. "Well, Mac," he says, "they weren't going to pass you. You're a black man, and they don't want any blacks practicing dentistry

---

[*]The Moulin Rouge re-opened under new ownership in 1957, but it never achieved the potential it had demonstrated during the first months of its operation.

in Nevada. Your grades were eighty-five and above in all of the operations that you did, higher than all but one of the other applicants. In my book you are a qualified dentist, and I told them that if they didn't pass you I was not going to pass another applicant as long as I was on the board." They had to have a unanimous vote at that time, and that meant that *nobody* would be getting a license . . . so they passed me.

I set up my practice at 812 West Bonanza Road, at the corner of Bonanza and "H" Street. It was in the black community, what we would call the Westside. Dr. West and I had bought houses on Wyatt Avenue in the new Berkeley Square subdivision. Unlike much of the rest of the Westside the subdivision had paved streets and lights and sewers and all that. Dr. West built a swimming pool behind his house and I built a pool behind mine.

My office was right next to the Moulin Rouge in a building with Dr. West. There was a restaurant next door, and a barber shop and an architectural firm. (Years later I bought the building.) After I opened I sat there for thirty days without having a patient, because everybody was going to other dentists, most of whom would only see blacks after hours. Dr. Faust was a very fine dentist, a German who had his office on Main Street. He would see blacks at any time and he would bill them. Other caucasian dentists would take black people only if they had cash, and then they would overcharge them . . . and they'd only take them after hours. They wouldn't let them in the door when white patients were in the waiting room.

Well, to get business I started staying open until seven o'clock at night. One night a caucasian called me from downtown. She had a severe toothache and needed immediate attention, so I told her to come in and I treated her. She was the secretary for the electricians union; she was so happy with the treatment she received from me that she took some of my cards and put one up on the board down there at the union office. A lot of people in the electricians union worked out at the nuclear test site, and after the secretary recommended me I began seeing many of them. They would get through with work at four, and by the time they would drive down to Las Vegas it was too late to go to another dentist.

Eventually I worked up a large clientele, and many of them were caucasians. Some white patients would come in, and when they discovered that I was black they would say, "Well, I don't know whether I could have a black man put his hand in my mouth." I would think one thing, but I would say, "Fine. You have a right to spend your money where you want. This is America." I still get some of that. We service three or four dental insurances, HMOs and PPOs and that type of thing, and these people come in and they find out that two of us are Afro-Americans. When they come in, they see all the caucasian people in the waiting room and they sit down and wait. Finally they go back and see that the dentist or hygienist is black, and some of them say, "Well, I'm sorry. I can't. I don't want you to work on my teeth."

It cuts the other way too. One time I had a patient in the chair when I was called to the phone. The guy was one of the largest paying patients I'd ever had—about six thousand dollars worth of dental work involving root canals and crowns and stuff. My phone was just to the back of the room, and he could overhear my end of the conversation. At that time I was president of the local NAACP, and we were working hard on the civil rights thing. I really got agitated on the phone, talking about integration and how bad white people were, and this and that. When the call was over the guy said, "Wait a minute, Doc. Just wait a minute. I must be stupid; I don't understand." He said, "Here I am sitting in your chair, paying you thousands of dollars, and you get on the phone and talk about how evil and dumb white folks are. What's your problem?"

I said, "I, ah . . . well . . . . "

But he couldn't just get up and walk out. He said, "OK, go ahead and finish the work."

Evidently Las Vegas was much less segregated before the Hoover Dam project and BMI attracted large numbers of blacks from the South seeking jobs. Black people lived downtown and there were black businesses on Second Street. They could go into some of the clubs, and they could shop and go to the movies. Some blacks even owned property downtown. In fact, the building the post office was in was owned by a black person who leased it to the postal service. But that all changed. For some reason Mr. Clark and the people who ran things in town decided to force the blacks out, harass them, get them to move over to the Westside. And that happened.

By the time I got to Las Vegas, it was rigidly segregated. You couldn't get into any of the places downtown to eat. You could go into the stores, but if you tried on clothing you couldn't put it back on the rack; you had to buy it. You couldn't go into any of the gaming joints. The only black people who worked in the hotels were porters, and you couldn't live anywhere other than the West Las Vegas area. Some black people bought property far outside town to the west, three or four acres, and they built houses out there, but it was difficult for a black person to rent a house anywhere in Las Vegas except on the Westside.

A Mrs. Shaw had kind of a little motel on the Westside, just north of Jackson Street, and she took in many of the visiting black entertainers; and Jodie Cannon, the fellow that owned the Cotton Club, had another house next to where he lived east of D Street, and the Mills Brothers and some of the important enter- tainers would stay with him. When I came to Las Vegas they were still doing that. Dr. West had two houses in Berkeley Square. He lived in one and rented the other out to black entertainers who were performing in segregated hotels on the Strip. I did the same, and that way I got to meet people like Joe Williams and his family . . . Lena Horne rented the house from me, and Count Basie. Duke Ellington and his band liked it because it had three bedrooms and a kitchen, and they could do their own cooking. You needed a kitchen, because restaurants all over town had signs up that they would not serve blacks. The only place where we could eat on the Strip was a deli named Foxy's, across from the Sahara Hotel, where the owner had a couple of booths for his black patrons—he'd let you come in and have sandwiches and things. But we had restaurants and businesses on the Westside, and two or three gaming joints. We had the Town Tavern, the Louisiana Club, the El Rio, the Cotton Club. And Oscar

Crozier had a small club over there, the El Morocco, that was doing great business.

Oscar Crozier had owned another joint, just a little hole in the wall which I had visited the first time I came out to Las Vegas; then he built the El Morocco, which was a big-time gaming joint. Oscar made the mistake of closing his first operation down before he had completed construction, thinking he could just reopen and keep operating as usual. But that violated the gaming law. If you close, you forfeit your license and have to go back and get permission to open again. C. D. Baker was mayor at that time, and when Oscar closed down, C. D. Baker kept him closed for three and a half to four years. Finally he let him reopen the place. I guess Oscar had gotten on the wrong side of some people.

10

Soon Somebody Nominated Me

I GREW UP WITH THE BELIEF that you had to fight for your rights and speak up and demand respect and equal treatment. As a boy I had been to political meetings and rallies with my mother, who was quite an activist, and I had heard her blast whites and everybody else. Then at the University of Detroit I got involved with the NAACP, and I've been a member ever since.

My mother had talked about conditions in the South, and I experienced them firsthand when I attended Meharry Medical College. When we went to the movies we had to sit in the balcony, and in general we were just segregated out of being able to do a lot of things, so we stayed on campus and read about how bad white folks were and about black folks being lynched and that type of thing.[*] And then my stint in the army, facing all the segregation that the military had at that time . . . . I decided to actively try to change things; decided that was what to do.

In Detroit after the war I resumed my association with the NAACP. My friends were involved too, and we demonstrated and did other things in the city, because segregation was in Detroit's system. Charles Diggs, Jr. was a leader and a friend of mine. He had been in the civil rights movement at Fisk University while I was at Meharry Medical College. (Fisk is right across the street from Meharry in Nashville.) Diggs lived in the black community in Detroit, where his father owned one of the largest mortuaries in the city, and he was later elected to Congress from that district. He became a forthright, courageous representative who tried to do all he could to get civil rights legislation passed.

I was the second black professional to come to the state of Nevada; Dr. West was the first. Shortly after my arrival I started attending local NAACP meetings. Dave Hoggard was president when I joined. Woodrow Wilson had been president before that, and Mrs. Lubertha Johnson had been president before him. Back before her, Arthur McCants was instrumental in starting the NAACP in Las Vegas by writing about the difficulty black people had getting jobs at the Boulder Dam project. He helped

---

[*]Many whites are unaware that lynching of blacks by white mobs was a frequent occurrence well into the twentieth century. In 1952 the Tuskegee Institute reported no lynchings for the first time in seventy-one years. For a more detailed analysis see W. Fitzhugh Brundage, *Lynching in the New South: Georgia and Virginia, 1880-1930* (Chicago: University of Illinois Press, 1993).

organize an NAACP branch to try to get jobs for blacks at the dam, and it just went from there. Dave Hoggard, Woodrow Wilson, and Mrs. Johnson did a great job of fighting for the rights of blacks. Then there was Donald Clark, who was just out of the army and was an assistant pastor of a ministry church. And we had Emory Ward, who was a brother school teacher at that time, and Dr. West, Bob Bailey, and Clarence Ray, who was a real old timer . . . those were the most prominent members in the organization.

We also had about ten or twelve white members, and some of them were on the executive board. George Rudiak was a caucasian attorney who belonged to the branch—he'd been in the state assembly and was one of the first to introduce a civil rights bill and a fair housing bill.* George Brookman's wife, Eileen, was also a caucasian member of our executive board, and she was later elected to the legislature; and we had a caucasian fellow on the board who was an insurance agent.

I was elected president of the Las Vegas NAACP after attending only a few meetings. I'd been talking and carrying on about all the segregation in Las Vegas, and soon somebody nominated me to be president of the branch. Boom! That was it. I served three consecutive one-year terms and two two-year terms. (When I was first elected we had a one-year term and then you got re-

---

*In 1953 Assemblyman George Rudiak introduced A.B. 248, "An act concerning the rights of citizens in places of public accommodation or amusement." The assembly voted to indefinitely postpone the bill, which would have made discrimination on the basis of race, color or creed punishable by a fine of $100 or imprisonment.

elected; then the national office changed the term to two years.)

Our executive board during the 1950s could number as many as twenty people. The president and the board met every week to go over issues and plan fund raisers. Mrs. Lubertha Johnson and her husband had a little vacant building right next to their grocery store, and at first we would meet in there; then a federal credit union was established on the Westside and we would meet there. Monthly meetings of the general membership were rotated from one church to another.

At the monthly meeting the president would bring reports before the general membership on issues and proposed actions, and request them to give us their support to do these things. We would also elect delegates to the annual meeting of the national NAACP. After my election we decided that a boycott of two local dairies would be our first project. (They were selling a lot of milk on the Westside, but they wouldn't employ blacks.) Then we started a campaign to get the NAACP into the churches. Churches in the black community are the largest groups of assembled people, and we would send members out to the churches to speak to them and raise issues.

We kept abreast of national issues by reading the black newspapers. The *Pittsburgh Courier*, which was an outstanding newspaper, was shipped all over the country; and there was one from Baltimore, and there were others that we subscribed to. We started our own black newspaper around 1957 and called it *The Missile*. David Hoggard and I published it out of the NAACP office—the money to run it came out of our pockets and from the

NAACP treasury. Our paper wasn't just about civil rights issues; it carried a lot of news about what was going on in the community.

We published *The Missile* once a week, on Saturday. One difficulty we had was that when we tried to get advertising from the caucasian stores on the Westside, they wouldn't give it to us, because they wanted their ads to go in on Wednesday. We would reprint articles or excerpts from the national black newspapers, add local stories, paste it all up, and then we had to send it out of state at first to have it printed. Finally the fellow who had the *Valley Times* started printing our paper for us. We did this for about a year and a half, and then we just couldn't do it anymore—couldn't keep giving it the time and money that it required.

Dr. West took over *The Missile* and changed its name to *The Voice*. He could write off the paper's expenses, and he had enough money to hire people to do the work. Dr. West kept *The Voice* for six or seven years. When he got sick before his death he sold it to a fellow named Brown, another Afro-American, and he and his wife ran it for a while. Now someone else has it. It's real good now.

The burning issue was segregation in jobs and housing and public accommodations, and the first thing I took on after I became president was a jobs issue. Anderson Dairy and Highland Dairy were delivering milk to the Westside—caucasians delivering milk in the black community. We asked them if they would hire blacks to deliver in our area and they said no. So we had a meeting and decided that we had to pick one of those dairies to serve us so we could boycott the other one. Anderson dairy was the larger one, so we attacked Highland Dairy first, and all of the people on the Westside who were buying milk from Highland discontinued the service. We kept that boycott on until they went out of business. And we got Reverend Clark the job of driving the Anderson Dairy truck that delivered milk in the black community.

We also boycotted some gaming clubs in West Las Vegas that were owned by whites and a Chinese fellow named Louie. The Louisiana Club, the Rio, and . . . . We wanted them to hire more blacks and pay them the same as their white employees. The boycott was pretty effective, and then some white dealers asked me to be the executive director of a union for them. They wanted to negotiate with the casinos to get higher wages, medical benefits, and that type of thing. I said I would. They offered to have each of the dealers pay me five dollars a month. I said, "That's fine. But you know, in order to have a union you have to have some backbone. Now, if I call a strike, you guys have to walk out; and you have to give me some type of protection as your executive director, or I'm going to wind up in Lake Mead somewhere."

They said, "We can't go out on strike."

I said, "Well, hell. You don't need me as your executive director then. Forget it."

After a couple of years we felt that we had done as much as we could do through boycotting and browbeating people to give us jobs and that type of thing. We decided to move into politics, figuring that we needed political muscle to get what we wanted. The NAACP

The first Freedom Fund banquet, Las Vegas Convention Center Gold Room, 1958. Left to right: Dr. James B. McMillan, Terea Hall Pittman (regional director of the NAACP), Dr. Charles I. West presenting an award to Woodrow Wilson.

couldn't be involved in partisan politics, so Dr. West and I formed the Nevada League of Voters. (This was mostly an Afro-American organization, but whites belonged to it too.) Our first attempt at election politics came in about 1958 or so. We ran Helen Lamb Crozier for the state board of education. We selected her because she had the Lamb middle name, she was a light-mulatto type lady with Indian type hair, and she looked good on the posters that we put up. Lots of voters thought that she was related to the politically powerful Lamb family. To my knowledge she was the first Afro-American elected to a position on the state board of education.

We also ran Reverend Leo Johnson for the hospital board. Since he was a minister we figured that he would probably get elected too, and he only lost the damned thing by ten votes. And we ran Dr. West for a seat on the city council. He made it through the primary, but he lost in the general. Joe Neal also ran for an office at that time, his first stab at politics. We had a big old wagon on the Westside, and all our politicians came up on the thing and made speeches, and people came to hear them.

In the 1958 mayor's race Oran Gragson was running against Wendell Bunker, a prominent Mormon. Some of the older black people knew Bunker; they had had some access to him. He had never done or said anything to make anyone believe that we would benefit from his election, but we supported him anyway because of some bad information: Oran Gragson was a southerner, and a rumor went around that he had named his dog "Nigger".

All of the people in the NAACP were members of the Voter's League, so we just changed hats and we had a meeting. We decided to back Bunker. Then Gragson contacted our organization and said he wanted us to support him. He said he would be a good mayor and he'd help black people and be responsive to some of the things that we wanted. I went over to his house with a delegation, Bob Bailey and some others, and I turned him down. I said, "I'm sorry Mr. Gragson, the League has voted to support Mr. Bunker, and this is what we're going to do. I just wanted you to know where we stand, keep everything above board." He was sorry to hear this, but he said he understood.

The election came around and we voted solidly for Bunker. Gragson got only about three hundred votes from our district, but he won the election. The next day Oran Gragson went up and down Jackson Street shaking hands with black people, saying that as mayor he was going to be responsive to the black community and we would really understand what type of gentleman he was and how he was not a segregationist and was not prejudiced. (It turned out that he did have a black dog, but its name wasn't Nigger.) He even appointed some black people to positions in city government. In fact, he was the supporting power behind William Pearson being appointed to the city commission.

Gragson proved to be a good mayor, particularly in his first term. The big time politicians in the city told him there were things that he just couldn't and shouldn't do, but he was always responsive to the black community, had black friends and made sure he did not exhibit any type of prejudice. Oran was eventually inducted into the Black Hall of Fame at the Moulin Rouge. After knowing him over thirty years, I don't think there was any prejudice in him. His administration was good for the black population of Las Vegas.

We did everything we could to influence white politicians to do the right thing, but there weren't many of them like Oran Gragson. We invited Senator George Malone over to talk to the NAACP—questioned him about civil rights and about his position on Senate Rule 22, the one to stop filibustering. He was a bigot who was playing politics with the southerners in the Senate. That was his game. Senator Alan Bible was a diplomat, a gentleman who talked out of both sides of his mouth and never did anything for us. We had him come over to meetings and he would pacify us and promise different things, but nothing ever happened. Walter Baring was conservative to the bone; there was just nothing that we could ever get him to do for black people. He came over to the Westside, wrapped himself in the flag, talked about what an American he was. We fought him to the end. We talked to him, talked about him, talked against him, and voted against him, but never could we move him at all.

And Howard Cannon . . . . Before I came to Las Vegas the NAACP had drawn up a resolution asking for the elimination of discrimination. They wanted Howard Cannon as city attorney to put it before the city council, but he wouldn't do it. He tore it up. He was just one of the "good old boys," and he never did do anything for civil rights or for black people that was visible. Cannon was elected to the United States Senate in 1958, and during his first term he skirted a vote about desegregation of schools; he wouldn't vote on it. Years later

Harry Claiborne and I ran against him for his senate seat in a primary, and my position was that he was a segregationist. Claiborne took up the banner also, and we both got defeated. The odd thing about it is that I received more votes up north and in the cow counties than I did in Las Vegas, and I don't know why—maybe it was because I had answered questionnaires from those people about desert land and ranches and these things, which I think they wanted to hear. We had a pretty nice campaign going, but I didn't have any money: I had homemade signs and Cannon had all the money in the world.[*]

Lack of money was the biggest weakness in all our campaigns . . . that and not fully realizing the extent to which money drives politics. Since we couldn't afford paid advertisements, we would try to entice television stations to report on our candidates, try to get a story on the radio and that type of stuff. With our white friends we'd go to white churches, and the white people who belonged to the NAACP would invite us to speak to their organizations. The Jewish synagogue would invite you to talk; the unions would help. We would solicit the culinary union and beg and borrow money to make some signs up. In the end we didn't win many votes, but our participation in the elections had a positive influence on some of the victors.

In 1958 most of our campaigning was done in black churches and out in the black community. Ninety

---

[*]For a more sympathetic treatment of Senator Howard Cannon's record on civil rights see A. Costandina Titus, "Howard Cannon, the Senate and Civil Rights Legislation, 1959-1968," *Nevada Historical Society Quarterly* 33:4 (Winter 1990), 13-29.

percent of the churches supported our political agenda—
they worked religiously with us to try to get our people
elected, and even though we lost most of the elections,
the community was together. As the years went by,
however, and issues got more critical, and we started
talking about picketing places in the cause of ending
segregation, some of the ministers and their churches
began pulling back. They thought the Ku Klux Klan
might come in and burn up the community. They
thought that maybe the white people would gather
together with guns and come over to the Westside
fighting, and a lot of people feared for their safety. Civil
rights workers must do like Martin Luther King did:
when they march, although they say it's non-violent, they
have to know that they're going to get arrested or hit
over the head, and somebody may die. Those are
possibilities that active people in the community must
accept for progress in civil rights, and a lot of people are
afraid to do that. They may support you from the
background by donating money or doing other things to
help, but they will not participate or march.

When I came to Las Vegas Mike O'Callaghan was a
Henderson school teacher. He had lost a leg in combat in
the Korean War, and he was a popular person. I had
known Mike for several years when he invited our
NAACP branch to meet a group of concerned citizens—
Christians and Jews, blacks and whites—that used to
meet at the YMCA to try to do something about segregation and unequal opportunities. Mike was president of
this particular group, and he had a folder that he let me
look at that listed the names of the officers and the board

of directors. Many of them were connected to hotel-
casinos. I touched Dave Hoggard on the arm and showed
him the list. He laughed. I said, "Well, we'll fix this damn
thing."

When the meeting started I spoke up and said,
"Mike, I think you're wasting our time here. You're the
executive director of this organization and your board of
directors includes the presidents of the Sands, the Desert
Inn, and other segregated hotels. Instead of having these
meetings and talking about civil rights and eliminating
discrimination and prejudice in this city, all you've got to
do is call your board together and say, 'Hey, this is
wrong. Just stop this discrimination and let everybody go
into your hotels.' Until you do this," I said, "you're
wasting our time."

Mike said, "Well, I don't think I can do this. I mean,
these are people who . . . blah, blah, blah." Same old
verbiage.

I said, "Come on fellows; let's go." So all the black
people got up and walked out of the meeting.

From that time on, I never had any more conversation with Mike until we met at a dinner when he was
running for lieutenant governor. That was ten years later
and we kind of worked for him at that time. When he
became governor, he was decent with us. He appointed
blacks to positions and he was responsive to the NAACP.
Mike's an honorable man who would make a decision
and stick to it. He wouldn't hide; he wouldn't finesse
you. He'd say, "I don't like this bill and I'm not signing
it, period."

Mike O'Callaghan was a tough guy and he still is,
but you could talk to him. He's a hot-tempered fellow,

and we had confrontations all the time. He'd let me know what was on his mind, and as rough as he was, maybe he gave the wrong impression sometimes. He didn't have any prejudice in his heart; but, you know . . . white people in politics, they have to work both sides of the fence.

11

Thirty Days to Respond

I
T WAS 1960. Oran Gragson was mayor and I was president of the NAACP. We had the Voter's League. Throughout the country there were sit-ins, and in the South people were fighting to eliminate discrimination.* The national NAACP office sent out correspondence to the presidents of all the branches saying that each branch should do everything possible to eliminate all vestiges of discrimination in its region. As I read it I asked myself, "What can we do to *really* start a movement here to eliminate segregation?"

---

*On February 1, 1960, four African-American students from the North Carolina Agricultural and Technical College in Greensboro, N. C., protested segregation at the downtown Woolworth department store by taking seats at the lunch counter and refusing to move. This protest touched off similar demonstrations in nearly two hundred cities. On March 19 San Antonio, Texas, became the first major southern city to desegregate its lunch counters.

Dave Hoggard and I got together that night and talked about it. I said, "Dave, we're going to write a letter to the mayor, tell him we've received instructions from national headquarters to take action against segregation in this community. I'm going to give him thirty days to respond, thirty days to tell us what he can do to help eliminate discrimination in the city of Las Vegas." We wrote the letter and I sent it to the mayor's office. I didn't expect an immediate response, but I thought that the tone of the letter might shake up white people, get them to think that we were stirred up and that we might actually do something this time. Three or four days later Alan Jarlson, a reporter for the *Sun* who worked city hall, was in the mayor's office. He saw the letter and called me and said he wanted to use it as the basis for a story, to get the news out. I said, "Well, good. Be my guest."

At that time most of the newspaper people and the television and radio people were tight with the establishment in this town. Nothing got out that would rock the boat. Hank Greenspun, the editor and publisher of the *Sun*, was the exception, and he was our early salvation. Greenspun loaded his "Where I Stand" columns with civil rights issues. In contrast the *Review-Journal*, which John Cahlan and his brother Al ran, never had anything good to say about blacks or eliminating segregation; in fact some people believe that the *R-J* went so far as to deliberately cover news about blacks in a negative way. We were lucky that there were two papers. If it hadn't been for Hank Greenspun and his son we wouldn't have had a chance to get anything in front of the public. Greenspun ran Jarlson's story the next day, and all of Las Vegas knew that the NAACP was threatening a boycott if something wasn't done immediately to end discrimination.

There was a national radio program broadcast from the Fremont Hotel, and this guy took the newspaper story and put it out that night on the radio: "The NAACP threatens a boycott on the Las Vegas Strip in thirty days if there is no response to their request to negotiate a desegregation agreement." When that went out on radio throughout the United States, all hell broke loose. Radio and television stations and newspapers everywhere picked it up. This was a tremendous story, to have this type of thing happen in Las Vegas, the convention city of the United States. Our local politicians *had* to start doing something.

I was dumbfounded by what had happened. Who would ever have thought that our letter could cause this much trouble? I was just as happy as I could be, and most of the black community was happy, walking around talking about it on their jobs and what have you. But some people were frightened and some of the ministers were frightened, saying that if we went and started a disturbance on the Strip, our side of town could wind up being burned down. But I stayed forceful, and the common people didn't want to hear that crap even if their ministers were speaking it. The ministers were saying, "Go easy, Mac. Go slow," but they did work with us from the very beginning. We even had meetings in the churches to plan our tactics, and this went on for several weeks.

Shortly after the news broke I had a meeting with Oran Gragson and Reed Whipple in my office. They tried to convince me to call off the demonstration, saying that it wouldn't be good for the city and the county, and they promised to be much more responsive to the black community in the future with city jobs and so forth. Reed Whipple, who was with the First National Bank at that time, said he would see to it that blacks could get loans to buy houses and start businesses and this and that. But they claimed they didn't have the power to do anything about segregation in the hotels and casinos and elsewhere. I turned them down. The demonstration was still on.

After the mayor and Whipple met with me there was no other movement to solve this thing. I'm wondering what in the hell I'm going to do now. I was getting death threats, telephone calls, letters, Ku Klux Klan people . . . my kids would answer the phone and they would wake up screaming at night because people threatened to throw bombs in the house. Bob Bailey and a group of men in the black community walked and stood guard around my house for ten days to make sure that we didn't have any fire bombing or shooting or anything like that.

After I turned down Gragson and Whipple, I had just ten days left to organize the demonstration. I'm threatening to have people picket with signs, people walking on the strip, blocking traffic, going into hotels, being arrested precisely thirty days from the date I had sent the letter. It didn't look like we could pull it off. We were having pep rallies in the churches, and the press and television people would cover these—we would make inflammatory statements about what we were going to do and how bad it was going to be. But that was all I had going for me. I didn't have any plans made for the march; I didn't have any groups volunteering to go into the hotels and get arrested and maybe get hit over the head . . . . I'm hanging. I'm about to be out there with nothing covering my naked ass. I'm thinking I might have to leave town, because I'm going to fall on my face: "This isn't going to happen. These people are *not* going to march, and we're going to be ruined forever in this town." The only thing that I had going for me was that the caucasians had not faced this type of thing before and they really didn't know what was going to happen. They were afraid.

Then we got a break. Oscar Crozier called me up. He'd been in touch with some of the underworld people that was involved in running the Strip hotels. He said, "I want to talk to you, man."

I said, "OK, come on by the house."

Oscar told me that the people who owned some of these hotels had flown in to Las Vegas and had a meeting: "They said they want to know what you're about—this boycott, this marching and all of this. They told me to tell you to cool it or you might be found floating face down in Lake Mead."

I said, "Oscar, they can't get off that easy. Tell these people that I'm not a gambler. I don't have any money. I'm not trying to cut into their business. All I'm trying to do is make this a cosmopolitan city, and that will make more money for them. You tell them that and let me know what they say." I was almost ready to throw in the towel. If he had come back to me and said, "Man, they said no. You better cut this crap out," I would have peeked at my hole card.

A couple of days later Oscar called again. "Mac," he said, "it's OK. They're going to make their people let blacks stay in the hotels. They're going to integrate this town. You can make the announcement that this thing has been settled and that there will be no more discrimination in public accommodations. Black people can go into restaurants and stay at hotels and gamble and eat and everything else." He told me that what I had to do was call the Desert Inn and ask for Mr. Taylor, who was running the place for Moe Dalitz at that time. "He will tell you that they have given you the final OK."

I said, "I'm not going to make any announcement until a couple of days before the deadline we gave the city."

Oscar said, "That's OK."

After I got the information from Crozier, three ministers came into the office and said, "Mac, we just can't support you any longer. You're going to get our town burned down. You have to call off this march."

I said, "You mean to tell me you're going to leave me hanging out here like that?"

They said, "We don't care, we don't want you to march. We can't support you."

These were prominent men in the community, but I had lost all respect for them. I told them, "Well, I want you guys to know that you don't have to worry about your town being burned down. It's all settled. Don't say anything about it until I tell you to."

Everything Oscar Crozier told me came true. I phoned Taylor and said, "I'm supposed to call you in regard to this march and demonstration that we're going to have. And you're supposed to tell me that I don't have to have the march, and that you have accepted all the terms that we have talked about."

Slowly he said, "Yes, that's correct. It's been settled. We have accepted your terms."

Hank Greenspun had been working behind the scenes with some hotel owners, and he and I called a meeting at the Moulin Rouge to announce the settlement. There were churches in West Las Vegas where we probably could have met, but I suggested that we should meet at a neutral site. The place wasn't fixed up or anything for it—chairs were all stacked up in the hall, and we just moved them around and pulled the table out and had the meeting. David Hoggard, Woodrow Wilson, Bob Bailey, Donald Clark and I were there for the NAACP. We had the justice of the peace, the sheriff, Governor Grant Sawyer, Oran Gragson . . . all of these people came, and the press was there. We announced that there would not be any demonstrations, because discrimination in hotels and public accommodations on the Strip had ended. The following day we formed teams of NAACP men and women to go out to the hotels to test them. And all the hotels accepted them. They could go to the tables to gamble; they could go to the restaurants and eat; they could make reservations for rooms.

Years later the Moulin Rouge was named a historic site because that's where we supposedly met to sign the agreement that segregation would be ended in the city of Las Vegas. But there was nothing signed, and politicians had nothing to do with it. Governor Grant Sawyer was in Washington talking with the Kennedys or whatever when this damn thing busted in the papers. He got on a plane and flew back here quick, and I met with him and told him it had all been settled. Other politicians were at our meeting to announce the agreement, but they had done nothing. All of their hand wringing and all of their rhetoric didn't mean anything: they didn't own the hotels; they didn't own the gaming joints; they didn't own the restaurants. This thing was settled by Oscar Crozier and a handful of powerful hotel owners, and politicians played almost no role in it.

The hotels had settled because it was good business to settle. They knew that some southerners wouldn't want to gamble at an integrated casino, but they also knew that they needed to make sure that the convention business stayed, and that white people would not boycott Las Vegas. Money moves the world. When these fellows realized that they weren't going to lose any money, that they might even make more, they were suddenly colorblind.

"The hotels settled because it was good business to settle." The March 1960 meeting at the Moulin Rouge to end segregation on the Las Vegas Strip. Dr. James B. McMillan is at the head of the table, flanked by Mayor Oran Gragson (l.) and Hank Greenspun (r.).

12

They Worked So Hard and
Risked So Much

W E HAD NEGOTIATED a settlement with the hotels on the Strip and most of the hotels and casinos in the downtown area. I say "most" because the Sal Sagev and Binion's Horseshoe Club weren't included—they didn't cooperate. We felt that this was really an affront to the NAACP and our agreement, and we decided to make an issue of it at the Sal Sagev, which was a white club on the corner of Fremont and Main Streets, owned by a man named Abe Miller. Dave Hoggard and I took Mr. Nolan Sharp down there. Sharp was a paraplegic in a wheelchair, and supposedly a veteran if I'm not mistaken. Surely they wouldn't refuse service to a poor black paraplegic veteran in a wheelchair! We figured that accompanying Mr. Sharp would get Dave and me in the club, and maybe that would do something for the cause. But the owner was hard nosed. They threw us out—threw the wheelchair and Dave and me out of the club and told us not to try to come in again.

Benny Binion being the strong man that he was in the community, the situation with his Horseshoe Club was different. And Binion had a black bodyguard, a man who had grown up in the woods with him in Texas. This guy was six foot six inches tall and weighed three hundred pounds. A rough, tough, bad cowboy! He had saved Binion's life back in Texas, and they were lifelong friends. Him being a security guard there and working . . . we felt that we just couldn't challenge Binion at that particular time. We let that alone. Binion took his own time hiring black people, and he took his own time letting black people in.

After we were thrown out of the Sal Sagev, Dave and I filed a complaint with the state Equal Rights Commission, which subpoenaed the owner. He refused to appear, and eventually the district court ruled that the commission didn't have subpoena power. We were frustrated, but we knew that the commission didn't have the power and we knew that they didn't have enough money to really pursue these things. What we were hoping was that the press would pick up on it and put a big picture in the paper and do a writeup about how ridiculous and inhumane this was. Over a year's time we kept fiddling with it, trying to make these things happen, but they never did.

Jimmy Gay was on our executive board; he was one of the first real important blacks in the community. I told him, "As NAACP people we need to have a meeting with the culinary union. This is getting ridiculous. All these black people that belong to the union, and we don't have black waiters and maitre d's and what have you. Well, we're going to find out why." So Jimmy arranged a meeting in our little office on Jackson Street. Al Bramlet was there (he was the big wheel in the culinary union), and Sarann Knight and two or three other people, and we had a confrontation about hiring blacks. I told Bramlet what a racist he was, and we really went to it. But I never could get them to move on making blacks maitre d's. Sarann Knight had power in that union, but although she and Bramlet were real close friends, I guess she never could pull it off.

I kept heckling Al Bramlet all the time from then on. He finally had someone run a background check on me in Detroit, and he found out about the incident with the magnesium furnace at the Ford factory. Everybody back there knew about it. It was on my record. So when he had me investigated, that came back. Then Bramlet started calling me a commie; he put it out that I was a communist.

In Nevada the two most prominent NAACP branches were in Reno and Las Vegas. Our civil rights movement in Las Vegas was more significant than the one in Reno, which wasn't doing anything. We got ours going first, got things settled, and then we went to Reno to see if we could help them. It was a tough task because Reno was so tight at that time, and some black Republicans up there wouldn't get behind us. Black Democrats and the NAACP people were staunch, dedicated workers, but the black Republicans would always say we were just outside agitators. They resented our presence—resented us if we went up to Reno, and resented us if we didn't, because they had their own agenda, and it was different from the NAACP's.

In the 1960s workers in the NAACP were dedicated and together, and there was never any friction between the Las Vegas and Reno groups. Eddie Scott and Joe Williams were quite active in Reno. Then there were the Woodards, husband and wife. He worked for the bus company; Bertha Woodard was president of the Reno NAACP for a while. The Reno people joined with us to attend meetings of the legislature and to picket the capitol and things like that. And they would send people down to Las Vegas to help us out on our local projects. Eddie Scott, Joe Williams, the Woodards, one of the ministers up there . . . they all worked to try to get it going in Reno, but it really didn't happen until years later. Finally it just slowly evolved politically, and now (1995) we have two black people elected to the legislature from the northern part of the state, both of them state senators.[*]

Reverend John L. Simmons was very active in the cause in Las Vegas. He had a church on the Westside; in fact he has a street named after him. He also had a church in Hawthorne, and he used to go up there once a month and work with Sarann Knight and the local NAACP people. Black churches historically have been in the forefront of helping black people achieve equal rights. The churches were places where blacks could come together in numbers to seek protection and help. In

---

[*]Bernice Martin Mathews and Rev. Maurice Washington.

the old days ministers would educate them and raise issues about discrimination and segregation and resistance, and there were some good ministers that went out and sacrificed their lives to help do this. Other ministers maybe had some different beliefs about politics and politicians . . . .

White politicians running for office would say to the black ministers, "OK, I need your support. I want to come to your church on a Sunday and talk to your congregation about my campaign, and I'll make a nice donation to your church." Some ministers would accept that donation but would still work with the NAACP and civil rights activist groups in the community. Other ministers felt that the politician could help the community more than the NAACP, and that they would have entree to him if they supported him and let him come to their church. If a politician came to a church and spoke to the congregation about his campaign and gave only fifty or a hundred dollars, the minister may have had a lot of demand on that politician.

The way I see it, it wasn't a matter of buying black ministers and their congregations. People decide for themselves whether they're going to be active in this political movement or on that political issue, and civil rights groups have to act even if they don't have all of the ministers behind them. While I was president of the NAACP I had tremendous cooperation from most of the black ministers, but there were some that did not agree with the things we were doing. We just had to go on and do our thing, and if those people didn't want to work with us, that was fine.

There were the ministers and Dave Hoggard and Lubertha Johnson and so many others who contributed to the success of the NAACP and the civil rights movement in Las Vegas . . . Charles Kellar, the second black attorney to pass the bar and start a practice in Las Vegas. After my last term in the 1960s as branch president, Kellar and Donald Clark worked together on the civil rights bill, and they did the suits on the schools and what have you.

Jimmy Gay, James Gay III, was already a very important man in Las Vegas when I arrived. He worked for the hotels. Whites thought very highly of Mr. Gay, and he could get blacks jobs. He did a lot of things for the black community. Jimmy was with our NAACP and the Valley View Golf Club when we were going to build a golf course. Some white people wanted to give us some land for the course, but we couldn't get enough money together to build it.

Aaron Williams worked at the test site and was active in the Democratic party in North Las Vegas. He and I had been in Detroit together. Williams was the first black elected to the Clark County Commission—served four years. In the end, when he didn't get re-elected, he made the statement that he was too light to be black and to represent black folks. He was a real light fellow, but he was an active worker in the community. He did a nice job.

We named our senior citizens project after Arthur McCants, who had initiated the first NAACP branch in Las Vegas during the days when blacks were having difficulty getting jobs on the construction of Boulder Dam. He was quite a man, quite an activist. So were the

Officers of the Valley View Golf Club, 1958. Left to right: James Gay III, Henry Moore, Jim Roberts, Andy Breuner, unidentified, Dr. James McMillan.

many others, men and women alike, who worked so hard and risked so much to end segregation in our city and state.

13

The Height of Our Strength

D URING HIS CAMPAIGN for governor of Nevada in 1958 Grant Sawyer and the people who were working for him met with us on the Westside. Sawyer and his supporters were being called the "Young Turks" by the press at that time. They had those flat-top haircuts. I thought Sawyer was a sincere young man who would help in any way that he could with issues of the NAACP and civil rights, so I signed on to support and to work with him.[*] From then on every time he was in the southern part of the state we would meet and I would get a chance to talk with him about his strategy and plans. Later he even became a patient of mine, came to my office to get his teeth cleaned and get an examination and

---

[*]For Grant Sawyer's recollection of his role in the struggle for civil rights in Nevada, see his oral history, *Hang Tough! Grant Sawyer: An Activist in the Governor's Mansion* (Reno: University of Nevada Oral History Program, 1993).

X-rays. By going to the only black dentist in the state he was showing people that he lived what he believed and talked.

Grant Sawyer was a good man, but he wasn't really a flaming liberal for civil rights. I think he figured that if he was to become governor of Nevada there were some things that he shouldn't do; but he did what he could for civil rights and still get elected and stay in power. Ralph Denton was Sawyer's campaign manager, and he did a terrific job. When Grant Sawyer was elected the first time, we got on the phone to tell him we wanted to meet to discuss the things we'd talked about during his campaign. He said OK, and we met with him at the Capitol shortly after he took office: Woodrow Wilson, Dave Hoggard, Don Clark, Andy Bruner and me. And the things that he had said he was going to do while campaigning, he did, starting with outlawing discrimination in state agencies in 1959. Then he proposed the creation of a Nevada Commission on Human Relations to investigate complaints about segregation in businesses and public accommodations. Now, that died in the senate. It got nowhere in 1959. But he tried his best.

In 1961 Governor Sawyer tried again—he asked for the creation of an Equal Rights Commission. This time he succeeded, but the bill that finally emerged from the senate created a commission with very little power to actually do anything. At the beginning of the legislative session we demonstrated at the state capitol in Carson City in support of Sawyer's bill and in protest of continuing segregation and employment discrimination in the private sector. We also had some productive meetings with the governor, made some recommendations about how he could better use the power of his office to push civil rights. I mean, the gaming commission reported to him. Hotel-casinos were the biggest sources of racial discrimination in the state, and the commission regulated them and controlled their licensing. Governor Sawyer began using that power to good effect.*

Bert Goldwater, a white Reno attorney, was named the first chairman of the Equal Rights Commission. When Goldwater resigned in the spring of 1962, Sawyer replaced him with Bob Bailey. Bob and I often talked about what was going on. He lamented that he couldn't get any subpoena powers, and there was nothing, really, that they could do but try to bring social pressure against the places and people that were still discriminating. Several years later, I believe it was in Governor Sawyer's second term, Charles Kellar and Donald Clark had grown impatient with the slow pace of desegregation. They wrote another civil rights bill that was introduced in the legislature. (I wasn't involved. By then I had resigned the presidency of the Las Vegas NAACP; I wasn't even on the executive board.) Kellar's bill would have created a civil rights commission with the power to seek injunctions against businesses that refused to desegregate—a violation would be a misdemeanor punishable with a fine and possibly imprisonment. That bill died in committee for lack of a sponsor, of course: it was too potent for the politicians. And the Equal Rights

---

*Gov. Sawyer and civil rights advocates had high hopes for this approach, but they were to be disappointed. In August, 1963, Nevada's attorney general, Harvey Dickerson, issued an opinion that the governor could not legally order the state's gaming regulatory agencies to establish nondiscriminatory policies.

Commission never did accomplish anything until it got
subpoena power and the federal EEOC came out. *Then*
it started to get some action.

The El Capitan in Hawthorne was notorious for
unyielding segregation and discrimination against blacks,
but it wasn't alone; it just happened to get in the papers.
All over the state there were blatant segregationists who
didn't think that they were doing anything wrong at all.
They felt that their establishments were their own, and
that they could do what they wanted to whoever came in.
Reno was particularly bad—segregation and discrimination were much worse there than in Las Vegas.

The 1960 Winter Olympics at Squaw Valley was a
big boon for Nevada in terms of publicity and money.
The Reno branch of the NAACP took the opportunity to
demonstrate, calling attention to the fact that all the
hotels, restaurants and casinos in Reno and at Lake
Tahoe were still segregated. Governor Sawyer wanted to
prevent bad publicity for Nevada, so he persuaded the
northern hotel people to take black guests during the
games, and the restaurants to serve blacks. But the
agreement was meaningless: there were no blacks
participating in the winter games—no black skiers or
skaters or bobsledders on the American team, and the
African countries didn't send any teams. And most of the
spectators were from the countries that participated. So
the hotel and restaurant people didn't do anything
courageous, because practically all of the people were
white anyway. But they made this big thing of it . . . .
We didn't care. Black athletes or no black athletes, we
didn't think an international event of that magnitude

should be held in a state that practiced racial discrimination. We continued to object to them having the winter games here.

In 1960 the state Democratic convention was held in Ely. This was an important convention for the Afro-American community. In Clark County for the first time we had elected all black delegates from our own precincts. We gathered together most of the ministers in the community, and we had Sarann Knight of the culinary union and Al Bramlet, and they were all there to support us. I think we had twenty or thirty votes, and there were some black delegates from the north as well. That gave us real voting power. When there's a conflict over issues, with whites disagreeing and splitting their vote, and we have a solid black vote, we can do our thing—Nevada's version of a black caucus. By voting as a group we supported Governor Sawyer and helped defeat quite a few motions that could have slowed the momentum of civil rights in Nevada. That was the height of our strength in the Democratic party and our movement at that time.

For the sake of solidarity at the convention I did something that turned out to be one of the biggest mistakes of my life. Ralph Denton had been elected to the state Democratic Party Committee, but he told me, "I think it's time to have an Afro-American on this committee. I'll resign and we'll appoint you." Initially I said OK; but Dr. West had been named a delegate to the national convention in California, and with my pending appointment to the state committee some of the brothers thought that we were trying to hog everything. To keep

the black coalition together I decided to turn the appointment down and give it to Reverend Prentiss Walker, a
black minister. That was a mistake.

Reverend Walker really didn't know how to handle
the position. He was as radical as I was, and no one to
mess with, so he was good for the things that we were
doing in Las Vegas; but there are times that you have to
be smooth and there are times that you have to negotiate
with people to get things done, and he didn't do us any
good. I should have said yes. That committee passed
on every appointment going to Washington, every
appointment going to the political conventions, every
appointment coming to Las Vegas from out of the
national office . . . .

When I say that Grant Sawyer was a man of his
word, he was. But when we got to the banking thing . . . .
During the campaign we told Sawyer that we blacks
needed to be involved in financing black housing and
business and so forth, because white banks weren't doing
it. We needed a savings and loan, a bank, a thrift association so we could do all of these things. And he said, "If
I get elected you can be sure that I'll give you the full
cooperation of state agencies and state government to get
started." The governor appointed the members of the
state banking commission, so when he sent us a letter
authorizing us to try to start a bank, we figured the
banking commission would OK it too.

You had to be capitalized for half a million dollars
before you could get your certificate to open up. I didn't
think we could raise half a million dollars, but whites
and blacks alike bought stock in our bank, and we did it.

We were jubilant. Tom Foley was our attorney, and we met in his office with the banking commissioner and our board of directors. We thought we were going to be given the certificate. The commissioner said, "OK, fellows, you've done a nice job. Tell you what I'm going to do: I'm going to demand that you raise *another* half million dollars because I don't want you to fail."

Now, the Nevada State Bank had gone into operation with half a million dollars capital. (They were a bank before us.) We had the same requirements, but Sawyer wouldn't force this man to give us our certificate. But I wouldn't give it up. I said, "OK, we'll go out and do it," and I went out to St. George, Utah, and borrowed half a million from a bank there at 6 percent interest. When we had this deal together we called the banking commissioner back down to Las Vegas. He looked at all our papers, went through them and said, "That's OK, that's OK, that's OK. You got a million dollars . . . . " The last thing he looked at was the contract that we'd signed with the bank in St. George. He threw that thing down and just raised hell. He said, "They charged you 6 percent for this money!"

I said, "Yes."

He said "Well, this deal's illegal. I'm not going to OK it." He turned the St. George bankers in to the federal bank people, and one of those guys was put off the board of his bank and damn near went to jail. We never did get our bank open. In the end we were unable to raise enough money to organize a savings and loan or a mortgage company either, nor could we work out partnerships that would enable us to do these things. That was in 1962 or '63, and we still don't have an Afro-American bank.

The bank thing was very important to us, and our failure to get something started has held our people back. In order for any race to survive, they have to deal with money—they must have capital, or access to it, to build a strong community. Civil rights were being advanced nationally and here in Nevada, but we were acting like fools, taking our money from the Westside and spending it downtown and in casinos, and we had nothing. If we could have started a bank controlled by blacks, not only would we be making loans to other black people, we would also be making loans to whites and making money from them. It wouldn't be just a one-way deal anymore.

When you're a mover in the world of banking and finance, you're accepted and you're a part of what's happening. But it's always been only caucasians in finance in this country. Know that! And the thing is, that keeps black people or Mexican people from being able to develop their communities. If we'd succeeded in establishing a bank and savings and loan and maybe a mortgage company, we could have financed construction and improvements on the Westside. We could have built good motels and casinos, and competed with many of the properties that white people had. Black tourists could've come to the Westside and stayed in first-class hotels, and we would have built businesses in the community. In fact, if we'd had access to capital, it's possible that the black Westside would be part of this mega-Strip business that's going on now. But we couldn't accomplish these things because the white establishment, the people that control the money, they knew that this was a *bad* thing

for them. You know: "Black people can have these civil
rights . . . they can do this and they can do that, but
don't let them get involved in finance and be able to have
capital and make money, because we've really got a lion
by the tail if that happens!"

After the integration of Las Vegas, and with federal
funds coming into the state and the city, a lot of black
businesses were developing. Several of us belonged to the
Las Vegas Chamber of Commerce, but we felt that we
would have more recognition if we formed a black
chamber. That way we could tackle black issues without
embarrassing caucasians, and then we could take them
to the Las Vegas chamber. To be effective we had to
have a large membership, so we decided to open our
chamber to school teachers and professionals as well as
business people.

Sarann Knight and myself, Bob Bailey, and two or
three others got together and incorporated the Nevada
Black Chamber of Commerce, which is still in operation.
It gives assistance to black businesses and it used to
handle a lot of the federal grants and things that came
into the city for minorities. The Latin Chamber of
Commerce and the North Las Vegas Chamber of
Commerce were formed later. I came to believe that we
didn't need all these chambers, really; we could have
accomplished more by being in the Las Vegas Chamber
of Commerce than we did by being independent.

14

Thank God For Lyndon Johnson

THE 1948 DEMOCRATIC national convention was of great interest to all blacks who were concerned about civil rights. A couple of big things happened. Hubert Humphrey's speech introduced a civil rights platform, but the southern segregationists split from the party and formed the Dixiecrats. The Dixiecrats would join with the Republicans over the years and defeat every type of civil rights legislation that came forward. Strong sentiment grew in the community for blacks not to be Democrats, because the national party was not really supportive of the vote that we gave them in the elections.

I never did leave the party, but I was often very disappointed with the Democrats, because even though they had the majority in the Senate and in the House, they weren't coming together to help us in our civil rights fight. Some northern Democrats were brave enough to at least mouth civil rights things and say to people that we need civil rights, but the southern senators were strictly racist. They'd been in the Senate for years, and through their seniority and positions as committee chairs they controlled the Senate; they knew how to manipulate it to defeat anything that the northern senators wanted.

In 1956 Eisenhower was reelected and got a surprisingly large number of black votes. There was a perception that he supported civil rights, but that Southern Democrats, and by extension the Democratic Congress, did not. Of course the Republicans weren't too happy about civil rights, either, but I think that Eisenhower, being in the army, seeing black soldiers serve their country, and seeing the rest of the world . . . . At least he tried to be a decent man and support the Constitution of the United States by sending troops to Little Rock in 1957. However, he didn't do much more. Knowing politics, knowing that he could not get it done, he just let it go. He was a non-entity, I think, in the black community; we were just living through his administration, hoping that something good would happen for us later.

Students at black colleges in the South had come to the realization that they had to do something, take some kind of action to get dignity and respect in society. In 1960 black students staged sit-in demonstrations at segregated lunch counters in Greensboro, North Carolina, sitting at the counters and demanding service and refusing to leave until they got it. They gave some drive to the civil rights movement. The Southern Christian Leadership Conference people gained energy from that, and things moved on. It got so tremendous that whites in the South fought the movement viciously with dogs and fire hoses and things. In the North, in Chicago, the Polish community was very opposed to renting houses to black people. They were just as bad as Southerners.

Everywhere in the country a black movement had started. Both national parties saw the trend. Congress may have been controlled by southern Democrats who were racists, but the rest of the Democratic party didn't share their views, and in the 1960 campaign they made civil rights a national issue. At the national convention they even went with a plank that asked for intervention by the Justice Department in civil rights cases. John F. Kennedy, who had identified himself with civil rights, was the party's nominee for president. During the campaign, as a political tactic, he wanted to intervene on behalf of Martin Luther King, who was in jail in Atlanta, and over a million pamphlets were printed to get the word out to black communities about Kennedy's support.[*] Nixon and the Republicans didn't do anything similar, and maybe that kind of contrasted the two parties—it certainly put many black people on the side of Kennedy. Nixon may have been in touch with civil rights here and there, but there was nothing to make us think that he'd be better than Kennedy. Here's a guy from Boston, a Catholic; he's talking about morals; he's a good-looking guy; and the Democratic party had moved forward with younger people coming in and talking

---

[*]In October 1960, Dr. Martin Luther King, Jr., was incarcerated at the Reidsville, Georgia, state prison, for his actions in a sit-in demonstration at Rich's department store in Atlanta, Georgia.

about civil rights. In 1960 blacks had no other place to go but the Democratic party.

The election was a cliffhanger, and a very narrow victory for John F. Kennedy. By then the mood of the country was changing, and whites were beginning to march in demonstrations with black people.[*] Finally the president had to say, "Well, hell, the Democratic party is really onto something. I've got to stay with this thing." I believe his commitment to civil rights was also strongly influenced by his brother. Bobby was in there walking around in the White House . . . . Bobby once said he was reluctant to be appointed attorney general, because then the president could say, "Well, I don't want you to do these things for civil rights." But we asked for him, and finally he was appointed, and this man was a tiger.

My recollection of John Kennedy, both as candidate and later as president is . . . I never did get the sense that this man would *fight* for civil rights. He was a tremendous speaker who talked about moral issues; but unlike his brother Bobby, he never said how we should make things happen. To me it seemed that he would go only as far as talk would take him—I didn't think he would control the Democratic party in Congress, get them to support civil rights legislation and actions. I think I was right about Kennedy, but during his brief time in office at least he was talking the good talk, and we had a national movement. At the same time television was

---

[*]In May, 1961, the Congress of Racial Equality (CORE) sent groups of civil rights activists calling themselves Freedom Riders into southern cities to protest the continuation of segregated rail and bus facilities. These had been declared unconstitutional the previous December in the U. S. Supreme Court's decision on *Boynton* v. *Virginia*.

exposing the awful things that happened to blacks who protested segregation—Bull Connor's dogs savagely biting and ripping at protesters, and black churches burning, and angry people . . . . The white man would see these things on his TV and say, "Well, this isn't our country. This can't be. This shouldn't be."*

Lyndon Johnson played politics when he was in the Senate, and he voted against some civil rights measures. That way he became a leader among the southern senators, who had great power: they were always reelected by their constituencies, and their longevity in the Senate meant that they chaired the committees and made committee appointments. They could stop proposed legislation at the committee level, and they could pressure northern Republicans—wouldn't put them on their committees and give them privileges if they didn't support the Dixie agenda. That's how the southern Democrats, and those people that they could convince to support them, ruled the country all of my life; and Lyndon Johnson was initially a leader in that whole

---

*From April through July, 1963, Birmingham, Alabama, was the site of massive civil rights demonstrations that led to confrontations with police. Eugene "Bull" Connor was the public safety commissioner of Birmingham, Alabama, and as the intensity of demonstrations escalated, Connor employed police dogs and fire hoses to drive back the protestors. Graphic photographs and television coverage produced national outrage at the police violence. One of those arrested in the demonstrations was Dr. Martin Luther King, Jr., whose "Letter from Birmingham Jail" further galvanized public opinion. On August 28, Dr. King delivered his stirring "I have a Dream" speech to over 200,000 peaceful demonstrators in front of the Lincoln Memorial in Washington, D.C.

southern Democrat thing. After *Brown* and Little Rock
we really thought that the Justice Department would be
our salvation—that on a lot of cases they'd just issue a
ruling that our civil rights were being violated—but that
didn't happen.* And Lyndon Johnson played a part in
keeping it going that way. He was not good for civil
rights when he was in the Senate.

When Johnson was running for the Democratic
nomination for president in 1960 he came to Las Vegas
to campaign. (Dr. West and *The Voice* were supporting
John F. Kennedy at the time: he was going to be "the
savior of the black community.") The Nevada Voters
League was there to meet him, Hank Greenspun was
there, Dave Hoggard and myself were there, and two or
three other Afro-Americans. I was president of both the
Nevada NAACP and the Nevada Voters League at the
time. So Johnson was there with his entourage. This
gentleman comes over and introduces himself. He says,
"I'm from Dallas, and I'm the press relations man for

---

*In its 1954 decision in *Brown* v. *The Board of Education* (of
Topeka, Kansas), the Supreme Court ruled that racially segregated
public schools were inherently unequal and thus unconstitutional,
thereby overturning the "separate but equal" doctrine which had been
legal bedrock for segregationist practices since *Plessy* v. *Ferguson*
(1896). Although *Brown* was a watershed decision, its consequences
were uneven, and resistance to its application was initially effective. For
example, at the insistence of Sen. Richard Russell (D-Ga.) the Civil
Rights Act of 1957 did not give the Justice Department the power to
seek federal injunctions in civil rights cases. Nonetheless, on September
24, 1957, President Eisenhower ordered federal troops to Central High
School in Little Rock, Arkansas, to enforce a federal court desegregation
order.

Senator Johnson. What are your views about supporting him for the presidency?"

I said, "He's the most bigoted bastard that I've ever known, and I wouldn't support him for dog catcher. You can go back and tell him that." Then I turned away to talk to some other people.

Shortly someone came up and touched me on the back. I turned around, and it was Lyndon Johnson. He stuck out his hand as he did—he had that type of handshake that when he shook your hand he wouldn't let it go until he'd made his point. He took my hand and he said, "I'm Senator Johnson, and I understand that you don't like me; that you said that I'm a bigot. I want to talk to you about that."

Here's this big fellow, over six feet tall standing there looking me in the face, gripping my hand. I said, "Well, that's fine. Yes, I said those things. I've followed your career in the Senate, and you voted against every civil rights issue that we had. You've done everything you could to see that black people stay second-class citizens."

"Yes, but I'm a changed man," he said. "I'm running for president of this great country. I think that I'm the person to lead it, and I'll tell you this—I will support the constitution of the United States and work for equal rights for *every* citizen of this country."

"How can you do that? You've been a bigot all your life."

He said, "Being president of the United States is bigger than anything else that I've ever attempted, and I will not do anything that is bad for this country. I tell you, I would be the best president that black people have ever had."

He went on like that for some time, and I was flabbergasted. He must have spent half an hour telling me how great he would be and how honest. He wanted me to understand that as a senator he sometimes looked like a bigot because he had to play politics to get what was best for his constituents, but I would be happy with what he would do for civil rights if he were elected president. The man was so sincere. It made sense to me that he could have one role as a senator and another role as president. He convinced me that he was fundamentally honest and ethical.

Of course Kennedy was elected president, and Johnson became his vice president. Some time in 1961 or early 1962 President Kennedy invited all the civil rights leaders throughout the country to Washington. In the reception line at the White House I met a friend of mine who had been appointed to the World Bank. He said, "McMillan! How are you? I heard you were a big civil rights man down in Las Vegas. You been raising hell?"

I said, "Well, you know, you hear the stories."

He turned to the vice president, who was standing next to him and said, "This is Dr. James B. McMillan, who now lives in Las Vegas. He's an old friend of mine from Detroit. We've known each other for years."

Johnson stuck out his hand. "Yes, I remember Dr. McMillan. We talked when I was in Las Vegas. Dr. McMillan," he says, "if I am ever elected president you will see the things happen that I promised you would happen."

Even after *Brown*, we hadn't seen the principles of equality and integration applied to accommodations, jobs, housing, loans and that type of thing, and I didn't foresee Afro-Americans getting to be real citizens in my lifetime. But when Johnson became president after Kennedy's assassination, he lived up to his promises. Most people hate him, I guess, but if it hadn't been for the Vietnam War this man would have gone down in history as one of the greatest presidents that we've had. He was surely the greatest president that black people ever had, because he went beyond *Brown* to pass civil rights legislation that other presidents didn't have the guts to fight for.[*] Thank God for Lyndon Johnson!

---

[*]Most notably the 1964 Civil Rights Act; the twenty-fourth amendment to the U.S. Constitution eliminating the poll tax; the Voting Rights Act of 1965; executive order 11246 authorizing federal agencies to enforce the 1964 Civil Rights Act; and the 1968 Civil Rights Act.

15

"What Did You Do . . . ?"

I OFFERED MY RESIGNATION to the NAACP after we had integrated the city. For personal reasons and because I needed to pay more attention to making a living, I decided that maybe it was just time for me not to be so involved anymore, so I resigned as president. But it was weird; I really didn't want to do it. I wrote a letter and brought it to an executive board meeting, opened the meeting and accepted the minutes and everything, and then I said, "Gentleman, I think that I should step down as president of our NAACP branch for the time being. I have a letter of resignation here . . . ." I figured that the board would refuse the letter, that they would say, "Oh, no, we want you to stay. We'll just tear this up." Well, Dave Hoggard, my best friend, said, "OK, Mac. We'll accept your resignation." I was shocked, but after making this gesture I *had* to resign. Donald Clark, the vice president, became president of the branch, and that's how he got involved in

meetings with Governor Sawyer and all the rest of it. And
Charles Kellar and Dr. West were on the executive board.
There must have been hidden resentment against me in
that close group. It just happened . . . . In your mind you
think, "Why?" Then you think, "Just forget it and go
ahead with your life."

Dave and I stayed friends and continued to work
together, but the reasons for the board accepting my
resignation remained unspoken. I may have been running a little roughshod over them. I didn't consult with
them very much, and I would do these confrontational
things, and I guess I just went wild with it. I was really
angry back then, and I'd been angry for a long time. For
a very long time. Most people who saw me on television
and read my statements in the Las Vegas papers thought
I was a bad man, and the way I talked, I guess hotel-
casino people and gangsters thought I was trying to
wreck their businesses. Maybe I should've had more fear
of the possible consequences of getting the white community stirred up. On our board Charles Kellar was an
attorney and he could protect himself, but Dr. West had
many caucasian patients in his practice, Dave worked at
the school district, Donald Clark had a job, and
Lubertha Johnson and her husband had a grocery
store—these guys may have been a little timid, a little
afraid to do certain things and afraid of the trouble I
might cause. They were probably relieved when I
submitted my resignation.

Donald Clark succeeded me as president of our
NAACP branch and Jim Anderson was the chairman of
the labor and industry committee. In 1963 they had been

negotiating with the powers that be about jobs, but there was no movement at all. Mr. Anderson came up with the idea that we should threaten to demonstrate and picket around the convention center where the Liston-Patterson heavyweight championship fight was to be held. This would let people from out of state know what our condition was. We got our groups together and went out to the convention center and actually formed our lines, but Hank Greenspun and Gov. Sawyer helped us negotiate a settlement before anything happened. We never did picket. We got some jobs, a few cocktail waitresses, dealers and things like that, but not enough.

Clark stayed several years as president and then Charles Kellar came on. He was an attorney and he started the movement of attacking the unions, trying to get jobs. He went to the National Labor Relations Board and accused the culinary union of being racist and not giving black people jobs. Later he forced the Nevada Resort Association to sign a consent decree and give the NAACP $75,000 to help train blacks to go into these jobs.[*] Well, the $75,000 got lost somewhere. I mean, money just did not go into training and it was not accounted for, and we never did get any more cooperation from the hotels.

Las Vegas was still not very large back then, had only a couple of high schools, and they had to bus

---

[*]On June 4, 1971, the United States Department of Justice filed a complaint charging various unions and casinos with violation of the 1964 Civil Rights Act. On the same day the organizations charged in the complaint signed a consent decree agreeing to refrain from engaging in activities that violated the law. None of the organizations admitted guilt.

everybody to those schools. But all black students, kindergarten through sixth grade, were being taught in our community. To get things started toward federally mandated integration we negotiated with the school district and superintendents of the schools, and we had three black teachers from our district go into white schools and teach so that white people would get used to us—we sacrificed three of our best teachers to let them teach white kids. Then when Charles Kellar became president of the NAACP branch, he filed suit in federal court to fully integrate the Las Vegas school system. (Kellar was very inventive.) While we negotiated, the whites got all up in arms, and they came up with what they called "sixth grade centers" to try to pacify us, get rid of the suit. They decided that if they shipped all white kids in the sixth grade into West Las Vegas for one year, then they could go back to their neighborhood schools the next year. At the same time they started busing some black students in grades one through five out of the community, out of their neighborhood schools to white schools, but they didn't bus white kids in the same grades into black schools.

Now we have what we call "prime six schools." Most black children go to those six schools that were in the segregated area; so they stay in neighborhood schools, the black kids. The black community agreed to that situation as an alternative to busing everybody out. We're also now using five magnet schools in the black community to help desegregate the system. A magnet school offers special subjects, special opportunities to attract students who wouldn't otherwise attend it. (For instance, the Academy of Performing Arts is a magnet for

Las Vegas High.) In Las Vegas, the grade school magnet schools are part of a federal program to entice whites into the black community. White people ship their kids in to attend these schools because they feel that they get a better education. The teachers get $2,000 more, and they're supposed to get more books.

A-Tech is the new scaled-down high school on the Westside. It has only 750 students, and they do computers and pre-law and a whole lot of other things like that. And the Mabel Hoggard School, which was a sixth grade center, is a computer school, first through sixth grade. The federal government says that you can only have thirty-five percent minorities in those schools. Sixty percent of the Las Vegas population is white, so that's the breakdown that the government decided on to integrate these magnet schools. It's a plan. I don't think it really does the thing that we need it to do, but at least it does integrate the school systems to that extent.

I continued to be elected to the executive board of our NAACP branch for another ten to fifteen years after my resignation, and I was again elected president for a two-year term around 1970 and another in 1982-83. But for a long time after I resigned I didn't attend a lot of the meetings, and I didn't go to Carson City with the others to put pressure on the governor and the legislature. I had only met with Grant Sawyer right after his election when we asked for a bank charter and a savings and loan charter and a person to be put on the boxing commission. He put Jimmy Gay on the boxing commission. Then we asked for the establishment of that Equal Rights Commission, and Governor Sawyer established that; and then he crossed us and made a caucasian the executive director of it.

In the early 1960s I ran for a seat on the Clark County Commission. We figured this was the most powerful part of local government, and it was time for us to have representation, so we decided to take a shot at it. I just chose the wrong spot. I filed against Harley Harmon. In my race we had myself, Harley Harmon, Paul Christensen's father, and an ex-FBI officer. Harmon was the most powerful man on the commission, but we were trying to knock him off—I don't know where we got the idea that we could; we thought maybe lightning would strike and we'd have a shot. Harmon's people met with the ex-FBI agent and made some type of deal with him and he resigned from the race. That left me and Harley and Christensen.

Then a guy came around to my office and offered to put twenty-five hundred dollars in cash on my desk if I would withdraw from the race. I told him, "This is not enough money. If I do this and it gets out, I'll have to leave town. I'd just have enough money to buy me an airline ticket to the Virgin Islands with a little left over. I wouldn't have anything to live on." I said, "I'll need a *lot* more money to pull out of this race!"

He knew I was pulling his chain, and I knew that I didn't have a chance to win. I contacted Harley and told him, "You know what I'm in the campaign for: equal rights and jobs for black people. If I lose the race, I hope you'll consider hiring black people for some of these county positions." He said he'd do that. He won that election, and three days later he appointed an Afro-American girl to a job in the county building, the first

Afro-American to work there. Harley went on to appoint a couple of other blacks to positions, but my campaign against him was the major part of his civil rights motivation.

I served on the Nevada State Board of Dental Examiners for twelve years. Governor O'Callaghan appointed me, and I served during his two terms and List's one term. I also served as the executive director of a committee that Governor List appointed to examine the reasons why blacks and other minorities weren't able to get small business loans and bonding and that type of thing. We went throughout the state holding hearings, and we submitted a report to the governor, and nothing ever happened.

In 1982 I was once again elected president of the Las Vegas branch of the NAACP and served a two-year term. The most notable thing we accomplished during that term was developing and building a 115-unit housing complex for the elderly and handicapped. Located at Harris and Eastern Avenues, it was sponsored by the NAACP National Housing Corporation, the Housing Authority of the City of Las Vegas, and the NAACP Nevada Housing Development Corporation in cooperation with the San Francisco Area and Regional Offices of the Department of Housing and Urban Development (HUD). We named it the "McCants Senior Citizens Apartments" after the Arthur McCants, the first president of the NAACP in Las Vegas.

In 1991 I ran for the city council seat that was also being sought by Frank Hawkins, among others. That was a hotly contested election. The police union and their people backed Hawkins. He had a big war chest, and they really got to me again. They did not want the two of us to go into the general election; they did not want both McMillan and Hawkins to run in the general election. John Moran campaigned hard against me. I spent $25,000 of my own money and got six hundred votes. In fact, I spent more money than I raised, so you know they had the pressure against me.

In all of the races, in all of my campaigns, I probably raised no more than a thousand dollars. I was spending my own money most of the time because I never did have a campaign manager who could go to the hotels and ask for support. During the council race I think Silver State gave me five hundred dollars and Bob Stupac gave me a thousand dollars, and that's about it. After I lost that race I ran for the Clark County school board in 1992 and was elected. In that race I spent thirty-five hundred dollars and got eleven thousand votes. About twenty-five cents a vote is what it costs to be elected to the school board.

The school district has a policy of naming new elementary schools after people in the community—white and black, Indians, school teachers, what have you—who have either done something for education or helped the city in other ways. People submit names to a committee which decides who will be honored. A few years ago they named one for me. The James B. McMillan School is on Lake Mead and Highway 95, just over in the white section of town. I think we have four schools named after African-Americans—McMillan, Hoggard, Parsons, and

Cox. I'm the first person to serve on the school board to have a school named after him.

When the school naming ceremony was held I was mingling among the students at the reception. One young man came up to me and said, "This school is named after you?"

"Yes, it is."

He said, "Well, what did you do to have a school named after you?"

I'm stunned. I don't know what to say. I said, "I can't tell you," and he laughed and we had our picture taken together. This was a very intelligent young man. It was sobering to have a youngster that age look me in the eye and ask that question.

With the tremendous growth in the population of Las Vegas, McMillan Elementary School soon had over a thousand students. It was overcrowded, so on the other side of the school grounds they built the Edith and Lloyd Katz Elementary School. The Katzes and I were sometimes in opposition during the civil rights movement, and now here we are, living together as schools.

16

We Don't Want to Live With the White Man

I'VE LONG WONDERED whether I did the right thing by turning down the offer Mayor Gragson and Reed Whipple made when we were threatening to demonstrate on the Strip in 1960. We had momentum, but the mood of the country at that time would have given us integration anyway in three or four years. By insisting that it happen *now*, I lost a great opportunity to get red lining stopped, and to be given loans and mortgages and jobs to placate us. That could have been the right way to go . . . opening up the city, eliminating segregation, didn't do anything but help the white establishment make more money. No economic benefit, nothing for black people. I thought that with a desegregated city, blacks would still go to black businesses and spend their money; but I soon saw how mistaken I was.

You can have all the civil rights you want, you know. You can get a job sweeping the floor downtown in a hotel or be a cocktail waitress, but if you don't have capital in your community . . . . I hate to say this, but in Las Vegas, through the success of the civil rights movement and our NAACP actions, we actually hurt the black population. When blacks were confined to the Westside, that's where their money stayed: we had five black gaming joints and two Chinese joints in our community that would hire black people, put them to work. All the money was going into black hands where we could develop the community—restaurants, stores, gaming, and things. Then when we got civil rights, and we could eat, shop and gamble anywhere, all this business moved to the white man. Before desegregation Jerry's Nugget was just a slot joint on the fringe of the black community, and now it's . . . . Jerry's Nugget didn't give us a damn thing. They got a lot of black business, but they only hired two or three black dealers for the whole operation. Here's how we lost all our money, all our capital: we were OK (sad to say this) as long as white people forced us to stay in our community, but when we solved that problem and tore the barrier down and could take our money and go, that's what we did. I'm saying that black businesses went under when we got our civil rights.

When desegregation finally came, and blacks began taking their money elsewhere, white businesses on the Westside were hurt too. The Westside had two clubs that were owned by Orientals, and it really didn't hurt my conscience at all that they lost all of their black business. In fact, I was happy. They hadn't been doing anything to help blacks anyway except hiring a few, and they were taking the money and sending it to San Francisco or wherever it was. They weren't putting anything back in the black community. The black clubs were the ones that

I felt sorry for, and the grocery stores and little shops. I thought that desegregation would make the town different, and the atmosphere would be better if we could go anywhere we pleased. But for thirty years after we won our battle I didn't see any construction going on in west Las Vegas. So there's a downside to integration.

Jewish people throughout the United States were very close with Thurgood Marshall when he was on the Supreme Court. Working with him they formed the NAACP legal defense fund, which has millions of dollars at the national level. We generally hired local lawyers to advise us on what we could do. George Rudiak did good work for us at one time. He was Jewish, born in Russia, and his family came to the United States and finally moved to Las Vegas. He took the bar exam and passed it and was doing well here. Then he got involved in politics and was elected to the legislature. He was active with the NAACP and with other civil rights groups, and he submitted one of the first civil rights bills in the history of the Nevada legislature when he was elected. His bill lost by one vote, and then he was politically dead, because white people wouldn't support and elect him again. He was also instrumental in building Valley Hospital in later years.

Jews had long suffered from discrimination too. They had enough money to fight it and win, and Las Vegas had some outstanding Jews who were interested in helping blacks achieve desegregation. But caucasians are funny people. I mean, when it comes to putting the leather to the road, they stumble. Hank Greenspun was friends with black entertainers and what have you, and

when we started the integration movement he got on
board. He wrote good articles for us, but . . . .
Greenspun was a big wheel in this town. He was in with
all of these big hotel owners on the Strip—the guys who
owned the Desert Inn, the Sands, the Sahara—and he
was respected. Long before the events that led up to the
Moulin Rouge agreement he could have said to these
guys, "Hey, this is stupid. It's time to integrate." Like the
Sands Hotel: he was in with its operators, who did a few
little things, but they wouldn't accept integration into the
Sands. And there were others. Greenspun knew what was
happening with me and the pressures that I had on me,
and he never did say, "Hey, Mac, come on. Let's go meet
Moe Dalitz or Wilbur Clark or Jack Entratter, and we'll
sit down and talk about it."

The Jews that owned the hotels and things could
have helped us end this segregation years before. All they
had to do was let the barriers down, let everybody in and
treat everybody as equal citizens. But that didn't happen.
Jack Entratter was a nice guy. He was lenient and would
let black people he knew into his place—Dr. West and
some of the entertainers would go in. I guess you could
call Entratter a liberal type guy, but there was no forceful movement from the Jewish community to hold hands
with blacks, marching and doing this type of thing.

Nowadays, with the advent of Black Muslims in this
community, with their agenda, there's been a rift
between blacks and Jews; but people should stand up
and support the Muslims, because they're taking young
black men and teaching them pride and the work ethic
and how to dress . . . and they're no-nonsense people.
Louis Farrakhan has made some harsh statements about

the Jews that may be wrong; I don't know. Maybe that's the only way to get these people's attention. But I do feel that the Muslims are doing things that are necessary to achieve equal rights in this country. They're doing one hell of a job, and in support of them I went to Farrakhan's first meeting in Las Vegas and sat on the stage with him. Some of my Jewish friends didn't like that. Too bad. If we're going to follow the constitution, we give every person the right to free speech. Just like Farrakhan's people are talking about Jews and whites, Jews and whites can talk about Farrakhan. They both have that opportunity. That type of speech lets me see an individual for what he is, and I don't think that his speech can hurt me. He's not hitting me with his fists; he's not lynching me. And I think that intelligent people can look at him and say, "He's nuts. Forget him."

Bob Bailey was a Republican, Woodrow Wilson was a Republican, Dave Hoggard's wife was a Republican, and Reverend Clark was a Republican; but all were more dedicated to the civil rights movement than most other blacks in our community. These people joined the Republican party a long time ago—I guess their parents were Republicans. In Mississippi the Republican party was the party of choice for black people right after the Civil War, the party of Abraham Lincoln. In Las Vegas black Democrats and Republicans alike knew that unless we were together, we had no chance at all. We discussed issues, analyzed our chances . . . but Afro-American Republicans couldn't do anything that would threaten their party. They met with us, marched with us, supported us, and then they'd go to their Republican meetings and try to do what they could.

Black Republicans are a source of strength, and they can be very good for our interests. I mean, that lets people know that both parties are effective in the community: the Democrats can't just take us for granted, and the Republicans can see that they have a chance to pick up some votes. But black Republicans have to let the party know that being a Republican doesn't mean that you treat poor people bad or talk bad about black people.

I disagree with intelligent blacks like Clarence Thomas and some of these black newspaper columnists who have used the civil rights movement to go through Yale or Harvard and get degrees, but who sit down and write about how bad black people are and how good conservative white people are! They can't be that ignorant; that just blows my mind! And it blows my mind that Thomas gets on the Supreme Court (and he's supposedly an excellent lawyer), and something comes to him that denies the rights of blacks, and he votes for the white people. I don't understand that. We have these younger blacks that have gotten excellent educations, and they think that they did it by themselves. Poor black people marched and suffered and were beaten and jailed to make things better, and these guys don't realize that they should now contribute something back to us. I just don't understand it.

And I don't understand why people don't realize what the unions have accomplished for this country. People say, "Well, the unions are taking advantage of people. They want to redistribute the wealth," and that sort of thing. Beginning in 1935 I worked in factories for five dollars a day, no vacation, no sick leave, no retirement, not sure of a job . . . fired at the end of every car year and hired back at the beginning of the next. And to see the difference when I joined the union, to see wages at Ford go from five dollars a day to seven dollars an hour, to have job security, to have a vacation . . . . Unions made the American middle class.

The civil rights movement changed Afro-Americans in this country. It gave us pride. It gave us a chance to stand up and be seen, and to let people know that we were not going to take this treatment anymore; we were going to do something! This is the important part. And around 1960, with all the attention that segregation was getting, we began to see some change in many whites. They were ashamed. They felt it was wrong for United States citizens to be treated this way, and this is what it took to end segregation. We had to have caucasians go into the South and participate in the marches; we had to have white priests and bishops and politicians take a stand and make a statement. That turned public opinion to help the movement. But the *biggest* thing that happened was that the civil rights movement got blacks to stand up with pride, to say we're doing something for ourselves and we're doing something to right the wrongs and injustices in this country. The march on Washington and Martin Luther King's freedom speech . . . these were some of the greatest things that ever happened in this country.

I also appreciated Black Power.[*] That movement had a lot to do with getting blacks to stand up and take pride in themselves. It made black people wear their hair in Afros instead of trying to pattern after white folks and put grease on your hair and wear a stocking cap and pull it back straight. We used to think that white people's hair was perfect and god-given: we didn't know that white women had to use hot irons to make their hair curly; we didn't know that white men had to put spray on their hair to keep it in place. Among blacks, straightening the hair was known as "conking."[†] I never did conk, but when I was growing up I cut my hair short and put grease on it, and I used to wear a stocking cap to bed. I'd grease my hair up and pull it back under that cap—that made it straight, and it would stay that way the next day. Then you had to do it all over again. Some men still do that—I have a friend who's eighty-three years old and he still wears a stocking cap at night. The grease makes your hair slick but neat, I guess.

When "Afros" came in, you could comb your hair forward, cut it short, put grease on it, and it just stood up. You didn't have to worry about it, and it was beautiful for our women. In the old days they had these

---

[*]In 1960, the Student Nonviolent Coordinating Committee (SNCC) was organized at Shaw University in Raleigh, North Carolina. Its name notwithstanding, SNCC soon took an aggressive stance in demanding civil rights for blacks. Two of its chairmen, H. Rap Brown and Stokely Carmichael, became leaders of the emerging "Black Power" movement, which departed radically from the non-violent tradition of Dr. King and the NAACP.

[†]For an excellent analysis of "conking" and related behavior see Alex Haley, *The Autobiography of Malcolm X.*

damned straightening combs that Madam Walker came
out with. These were hot combs that blacks would use to
try to make their hair look like a white person's—they'd
pull their hair straight and put that hot comb to it, and
it looked like hell. At the same time caucasians were
wanting their hair curly. It's just that type of thing.

It was a shock to me when I first started seeing black
women with their hair cut short or wearing it in an Afro,
proud of it and walking proud. And black men wearing
Afros and saying, "Yes, I'm black." We stopped saying,
"My mother is white and my father was black," or, "I've
got some white in me." We started saying, "I'm black."
We were proud to use the word. When I was coming up
in high school and college and in the army that didn't
happen, but when the Black Power movement came, the
black race stood up and looked white people in the eye
and said, "Yes, I'm black. So what!"

I respect all the different approaches to getting rights
for black people. We needed each of them, and we need
them still. The Christian Leadership movement, based in
the South, motivating its congregations to get out and do
something . . . . * The NAACP used a different approach:
a non-violent movement led by lawyers who understood
what the system was, understood the law, understood
how to go to court to get the things we needed. And
Black Power reached out to other blacks to say, "Hey,
I'm a human being and I want to be treated like a human
being. Until that's understood, I have to stand up and

---

*The Southern Christian Leadership Conference (SCLC) was
organized in 1957 by Dr. Martin Luther King, Jr., Ralph Abernathy,
and others.

support and protect myself." Caucasians began to see that the Afro-American was not going to be submissive anymore; they would not be able to run over him.

The Black Power movement gave us pride in ourselves and in our race, but I disagreed with the fringe people who were talking about killing whites. They were like these militia groups that white people are doing now—no difference. When blacks were doing this stuff, J. Edgar Hoover spent millions of dollars tapping our phones and chasing us; now the government's not doing anything to these white militia people, even though they're much more vicious than we were. But it all comes around. And there's a big difference between radical Black Power groups and these militias: the militias are saying that the federal government is bad. We didn't say that the government was bad; we just said, "Well, we'll beat it in the street." We thought that the United States of America was the greatest place in the world, and we wanted to participate fully in all that it had to offer. These militias now are saying that the United States is bad and that we've got to tear it up or rewrite the constitution or some such crap. They blew up the federal building in Oklahoma City. That's what these people do to make their point.

You can have family values without having economic security. In the South, black Southern Baptists living in shacks and eating soup were still honest, open, and straightforward . . . not robbing people, not cheating them, and not doing anything wrong. My stepfather may have run a numbers game to support us, but you can operate a gaming business and not kill anybody and not cheat anybody and not steal anything and be honest. Nowadays, people are peddling dope and running prostitutes and robbing and killing each other, and the whites are hollering about black criminals. Well, the black criminals are killing black people. Does that make any sense? The white person says, "These black people are criminals. They're doing this, they're doing that, they're shooting people." Well, we're not killing white people. I mean, black criminals may be *robbing* whites, but that's a different ball game.

And the riots . . . it's stupid to have a riot in your own neighborhood and burn up all of your businesses. If we were going out into our neighborhoods and burning up the caucasians' stores and tearing them down because they didn't have black people working in them, I could agree with that. That may be wrong, but I can agree with it. We have a right to cleanse our neighborhoods. But if you want to make a statement, go into the white communities and tear them up! If you're going to get out of servitude and get out of slavery, you can't do anything by burning up your own places. You got to do something to hurt the other guy, the one that's putting you in slavery.

Maybe peaceful demonstrations can do it as well. Mahatma Ghandi did it in South Africa; but Jesus, look what he went through! All of the demonstrations and civil rights activities that I was involved in were peaceful—we never burned anything; nobody was ever hurt, nor did we ever intend to hurt anybody. We would've protected ourselves from being hurt, but we never even had to do that. Other people have pushed forward by blowing up places. People say, "Hey, we better do *something* here—what's happening now in this country is awful." You can't just stand by and say, "I'm only going to do peaceful demonstrations" while Bull Connor puts the dogs on you and beats the hell out of you and throws you in jail. Maybe you can gain your freedom by taking abuse in demonstrations until the white man's conscience gets the best of him, and he says, "OK, we're not doing this thing right." But that's a hell of a price to pay. Mahatma Ghandi and Martin Luther King didn't believe in fighting back. I believe in fighting back.

Politicians, and particularly Republicans, don't give a damn about the poor, but poor white people go for their game. If the poor white people and rednecks would get together with Mexicans and blacks, we could rule the country. We have the votes.

Since the abolition of slavery, the greatest thing that has happened for the Afro-American is the passage of the Voting Rights Act. At the time it took effect there were no black elected politicians in the South—no city commissioners, no mayors, no policemen, no firemen, no blacks on school boards. Today we have almost four thousand black elected officials, all stemming from this voting rights act and from the presidency of Lyndon Johnson. In fact, and it's something I never would have believed could happen, we now have a black mayor of Dallas. At a time when whites are claiming to be victims of "reverse discrimination," and affirmative action is going all to hell, white people get together with black people to elect a black mayor in Dallas. I don't understand this.

And Colin Powell: I never thought I'd see the day that caucasians would say that a black man would make a good president of the United States. They turned against Phil Gramm because he has an Asian wife, but if Powell is ever elected, the first lady of the United States of America will be black. I don't understand it. Colin Powell looks good, but he wasn't all that great in the Gulf War and he didn't do a hell of a lot of fighting in Vietnam. He didn't go to West Point; he came through the National Guard—he played the system, and I give him credit for that. He knew how to play the system. I'd be glad for white people to put him on the ticket. If he's elected I hope he's got enough sense to be a good president and not let white folks trick him.

I'm confused about what's really happening in this country: black Republicans elected, and black commentators writing for the papers, speaking against blacks, against affirmative action, getting it all mixed up. I'll be a Democrat the rest of my life, because I believe in human rights and equality. I believe all people in this country have the right to make a living. Republicans believe that too, but they're a little bit more selfish than Democrats—they're in the business of business, and black Republicans hurt their own kind by holding down wages and having white people make small wages too. Nonetheless, I think Afro-Americans should put more black folks in the Republican party.

Clarence Thomas is a Republican, and he's certainly black. That's what hurts. He's a house nigger, an Uncle Tom to the fifth degree, and I hope that he'll hurry up and get the hell off the Supreme Court some kind of way.

How can a man from Yale, educated in the Catholic faith, be against affirmative action and quotas in the schools when he got his education and his position through affirmative action? Guys like Thomas have the wrong idea . . . maybe they can't be *real* blacks when they're in the Republican party. They don't join the party and say, "Hey, you Republicans are wrong. You're discriminating against blacks." No, they have to get up and mouth what the white Republicans tell them to say, and turn against their own race.

There's no way in hell that Clarence Thomas sits up there on his court bench and thinks about his poor people in Georgia. And he should. He should think about how the white people treated his mother and father in Georgia, "and that was wrong and I want to remedy that wrong." His position should be, "I'm an educated black man and I'm going to read the law right, but I'm not going to degrade my black people just to make me a big man." But as far as the Anita Hill charges went, I think the sexual harassment thing is bullshit. It's getting out of hand, and not just with what happened to Clarence Thomas. There was also Senator Packwood, charged with doing things twenty years ago. That's ridiculous. Now they're talking about President Clinton, about something they say he did in Arkansas when he was running for governor years ago. Our public officials are wasting our time and our money trying to get rid of Clinton, trying to get rid of Packwood, trying to get rid of Clarence Thomas instead of concentrating on social security, health benefits, retirement benefits for people . . . . And then there's the environment, which is being wrecked. Why will white people of intelligence, from the best schools and supposedly with the best education, make such stupid decisions about the environment? Money?

Affirmative action is what the Afro-American community and all minorities need. Affirmative action does the job. How in the hell can white males be complaining when they've got 98 percent of the jobs? They're going to object when a few people who aren't white get moved up in the system? That's stupid. The lawyers use the phrase "reverse discrimination," and it makes no sense to me. I mean, my reasoning is poor, I guess. I can't understand what they're talking about, "reverse discrimination." You've got a fire department with 100 percent whites, and you get a qualified black and a qualified white applying for the job, and the man says, "I'm going to let this black man have this job because we don't have any blacks working in the department . . . . " That's discrimination? No, that's affirmative action.

We should follow the constitution, just that simple. If we follow the constitution, that eliminates all of this other stuff—whether you're black or brown, male or female . . . . Now some people are saying that affirmative action and quotas are unconstitutional, but caucasians should not have all the benefits to themselves, and the only reason they do is that they have barriers against minorities getting those jobs. That makes the difference. When those barriers no longer exist, we won't need affirmative action. We'll be equal, and that means that if I meet the criteria to be accepted into West Point, I get in; and once I'm in, the West Point people don't give me the silent treatment the way they did Benjamin Davis. Equality under the law means being treated like anyone else. Let me be able to compete with everybody else for jobs, for housing, for education. Equality should be an individual thing, and if individuals are equal we don't even have to think about groups.

Busing initially served the purpose of getting Afro-Americans in schools with caucasians and letting those two people see one another and see that they weren't savages or people that they couldn't get along with.[*] The only reason that we needed busing was that in the South and in some of the larger cities black children couldn't get an education if you didn't bus them to the white schools where all the money was, where all the books were, where all the good teachers were. Once it started we had a lot of obstacles to overcome, because a lot of the caucasian teachers treated black students poorly. In Las Vegas we were busing grades one through five to white schools, and the Afro-American kids would get off the bus and the white teacher would come to a white kid and put her arms around her and let the poor little black kid . . . he's lost trying to find his way in.

Busing served its purpose, but we've had a real turnabout now. A lot of blacks are saying, "I don't need integration if I can get the schools, money, and proper teachers to educate my kids." The thing that we're faced with on the school board now is that black people are

---

[*]In its 1971 decision in *Swann* v. *Charlotte-Mecklenburg Board of Education*, the United States Supreme Court had ruled that busing children to distant schools to achieve desegregation is constitutional.

saying, "I don't want my kids bused. I want them to get an education." I mean, we don't want to live with the white man. We don't want to join his clubs or visit him in his house. All we want is to be educated the same as everyone else. The same thing with housing: we don't care about who lives next door. It's a human being—we respect him, we want him to respect us. And we don't want to integrate as far as marriages are concerned. (Of course, I'm married to a white woman, but that's nothing to do with race. She's an individual, a person—we didn't see color when we met and fell in love with one another.)

I've tried to live a decent life and do a good job as a professional man and as a community activist; tried to overcome my failures and accept my successes as things that were earned, things that I worked hard to do. I made some mistakes along the way, no doubt about it, and I have no great legacy to leave behind. I'll just be happy if the city of Las Vegas knows that Jim McMillan came through and did his best. Since our Moulin Rouge agreement, you can see the progression, the forward movement in this city. There's still some segregation, some prejudice, but now we have many black professionals in Las Vegas: we have forty or fifty black physicians, and most of them are specialists; we have black people as vice-presidents of banks; and we have black lawyers. (In America it makes a difference when you have fifty black lawyers who can go to court to solve your problems . . . and we do.) We have six or seven black millionaires. We have blacks on the big golf courses, living in gated communities, belonging to all the clubs. That's the way it should be.

17

Marie is Caucasian

M ICKI (MY SECOND WIFE) and I divorced around 1962. Long after the Moulin Rouge Agreement, and after I had gotten the divorce, I went out to the Desert Inn with a friend of mine, a Mexican woman. We sat down in the lounge and ordered drinks. No problem. Then this guy came over to where we were sitting. He said, "Dr. McMillan, I'm Moe Dalitz."

"Oh, it's a pleasure to meet you."

He said, "You think you're a pretty smart guy, huh?"

"No," I said, "what do you mean?"

"You're pushing your luck. You make us integrate the place, and then you come in here with a white woman. I don't understand what you're trying to do."

"Well, I wanted to make sure that you guys were living up to your promises. As long as I'm being treated as just another citizen, there's no problem."

Dalitz had been joking and we were friends after that. When he later took over the Las Vegas Country Club, I'd go out to play golf, and if he was there we'd sit down and have a drink and talk and laugh. He was always a gentleman.

It wasn't long before I was married again. My third wife, Marie, was a patient of mine. Her husband was an engineer, and she worked as an administrative assistant out at the nuclear test site. One time she came in to see me for some dental work, and we flirted a little. She was wearing a Chinese-type dress, slit up one side, and as she walked down the hall to leave I let out a whistle and said, "Woo!" She laughed. After Marie got a divorce we started dating. We had things in common. She had a Jaguar and drove race cars, and I had a Corvette; and I had an airplane and she had an airplane. We went to ground school together, taking instruction to learn how to fly, and we flew airplanes together, danced, dined, went to shows, golf tournaments, horse races . . . . After about a year of this exceptional relationship, one night we slipped down to the Clark County Marriage Bureau at about two o'clock in the morning (it stayed open twenty-four hours a day) and picked up a marriage license.

Marie is caucasian. Being married to a white woman could have caused me problems in the black community, but we just decided to get married and do it our way, and I wouldn't accept any problems. I just went on doing my job and being an activist, fighting for black rights and equal treatment. My patients were both white and black; I hired both black girls and white girls for my office; I went about my business. I knew that there was some

"We had things in common. She had a Jaguar and drove race cars, and I had a Corvette." Marie Stever-Daley (above) and Dr. James McMillan (below), 1963.

cloud over me, that there was talk, but I didn't pay any attention to it. My wife knew it also. And she'd be around other whites who would talk about black people, not knowing that she was married to a black man, and she had to be able to overcome that and live with it.

Recently a black activist called me. She said, "You married a white woman. You got white kids. Your kids are dating white girls, and you don't want to do anything in the black community." First time I ever heard that—they may have been saying it behind my back all along, but it's not true. I must say that as long as we were in the black community they respected me and my wife, as we respected them. What happened after we left, I don't know. My wife had some very good friends in the black community, but she didn't spend a lot of time there because we had some business ventures when we first got married. We owned six apartment buildings and a trailer court, and she quit her job at the test site to help me run the trailer court and manage the apartments and stuff. She knocked on an apartment door one day to collect the rent, and the woman who opened it said, "You white bitch. Get out of here," and tried to pour hot oil on her. But we went about our business, doing our thing, not making a big issue of our marriage.

18

Follow Your Heart: Marie's Story

*D*R. *JAMES B. McMILLAN wed Marie Stever in
1964. Marie remembers the early, difficult years
of their interracial marriage and offers some
insight into the indomitable character of the man she
calls McMillan:*

My father and his twin brother were born on a large
farm or ranch in Missouri. Their family farmed, but their
father ("Old Benton" Stever) also bought horses and
mules for the U. S. Army and delivered them to Fort
Riley, Kansas, which at that time was the army's main
cavalry post. Sometimes he took the boys along with him.

My Dad joined the army and fought in France in
World War I, and after the war he migrated to
California, where he had relatives in the San Joaquin
Valley. He met my mother, Eva Marie Cash, at a high
school football game—she was a cheerleader, known at
that time as a "Rah-Rah Girl." (Mother went to high

school with the mother and father of Robert List, who was governor of Nevada from 1979 to 1983.) Because it was located in the midst of such rich agricultural land, Exeter, their home town, had more millionaires per capita than any other town in California back then.

My Mother's great, great grandmother, Hannah Cole, was named the "Pioneer Mother of Missouri." There is a bronze statue of her in St. Louis, commemorating her status as the first caucasian woman to cross the Mississippi River by covered wagon. After McMillan and I were married, my mother and Mac used to have heated discussions about their ancestors—his coming from slavery and hers coming from the Midwest where the Cashes, Coles and Youngers were cowboy bandits. They had lots of laughs about that.

I'm a Leo. I was born August 1, 1926, in Exeter, California, and I led a marvelous, marvelous childhood. We rode horses, hiked, camped, traveled, et cetera. My two brothers, Jim and Bob, were born after me. With his knowledge of refrigeration my father developed a meat market and deli in Carmel-by-the-Sea, and that's where I grew up—in a two story log house near the Mission San Carlos Borromeo where I sang in the choir. The market was so successful that Dad put another one in Salinas, in what they called a "drive-in market," which was a forerunner of modern shopping centers. During the Depression I can remember other people not having anything, but we always did, and it seemed like we had the best times of our lives.

During World War II we moved to San Leandro. My father worked at the Naval Supply Depot, doing refrigeration on the big ships carrying food overseas to our military operations, and my mother worked at the Caterpillar tractor company, where tanks were built for the war effort. I graduated from Hayward High School and went on to the University of California at Berkeley, where I led quite a sheltered life. The dormitories were all full at that time, and my parents wouldn't let me live off campus, so I rode back and forth from San Leandro to Berkeley with a professor of optometry. In 1945, after about a year and a half at Berkeley, I got married to an engineering student. We had two children, a daughter, Michelle, born in 1946 and a son, Jack, born in 1947.

While my children were young I continued to go to school and became a licensed audiometrist. Then we moved to Livermore where I was an administrative secretary for the University of California Radiation Laboratory. My husband was an electrical engineer there. Eventually he took a position with Edgerton, Germeshausen & Grier (EG&G), a company that did high-speed film photography for the radiation laboratory at Livermore and timing and firing of nuclear devices at the nuclear test sites in Nevada and at the Pacific proving grounds. For several years during the testing program we would visit Nevada. Then in 1959, when a position opened up with Holmes & Narver, Inc., the engineering and construction firm that ran the Nevada test site, I went to work there as an administrative assistant for Pat Ryan, the resident manager. I thought I was only going to be there for a year, but life changes, and I ended up marrying McMillan. I've been in Las Vegas ever since.

Out at the test site our company had a great number of survey crews, a lot of people working for them, and someone would always have some sort of a dental problem. I'd heard that there was this McMillan fellow in Las Vegas who was a very good dentist, and who was the only one who stayed open late so that people out at the test site could get in to see him after work. (The test site was geared up to full activity at that time, and we worked about eighty hours a week.) If someone asked if I knew of a dentist, I would always tell them about McMillan. During that time my brother Jim was staying with me, and one day he had a toothache. I recommended McMillan. He made an appointment with him and saw him and came back and said, "You're right; he's a good dentist. Why didn't you tell me he was black?" I said, "I didn't know he was black." Nobody had told me. They had just said how good he was, and how accommodating.

While I was working for the engineering firm my husband and I divorced, and then he died and I sent my children away to school in Europe. I'd long wanted to get a pilot's license, and finally about 1963 I had enough time off from my work to prepare for the FAA flying exams. I went to ground school out at the North Las Vegas Air Terminal, which at the time was called Thunderbird Field, and who should I meet out there but McMillan? He was studying to be a pilot too. The first time we saw each other, everything clicked; we just were in tune with each other's thoughts. We did wind triangles together and we talked about airplanes, and we liked cars. Of course, McMillan was from Detroit and he liked to talk about Detroit cars. I thought Detroit cars were for the birds, and I told him so—I called them "Detroit barges." He drove a Corvette, and I drove an XKE

Jaguar, and we'd go out and race in the desert after ground school. We just had the most marvelous time together, really enjoyed each other's company. Nobody ever hit it off like we did.

We started dating right away. Of course this was 1963, so when we were out together in public we drew lots of stares and strange looks. McMillan was always very careful about how we would enter restaurants and things, and I wasn't accustomed to that. He still has a tendency sometimes to . . . oh, he always uses the front door, but he's looking around to see who's there and how many blacks are working. I think he was trying to be protective of me. He had been married before, and I think they had had some problems with disapproving people. He didn't want me to go through any of that, and I never did. A lot of things happened to me out in public, but nothing that I couldn't handle myself—strange looks didn't bother me at all, because I really wasn't aware that he was black. Nor did I know he was so prominent. Every place we would go he would know everyone, and I was pleased that he would introduce me as his fiancee.

McMillan would take me to shows and horse races and championship boxing matches. I had never been to a big heavyweight fight before, and he always had the best seats, the best of everything, and we'd sit right down front in these marvelous seats. The first time he took me to one we went early and sat down, and I could watch everybody come in. At that time it was not like it is now: everybody dressed up to do things in Las Vegas. People had come from overseas and from New York and Detroit and Indianapolis, and there were all these black men in what looked like zoot suits. One would be dressed in light purple and one in pink and one in yellow, with big hats on and with girls on their arms. Well, it was the best show I had ever seen! I just couldn't get enough of it. It was like going to a stage show. McMillan didn't care much for my enthusiasm, but that was the first time after we got together that I was conscious of race. I was just brought up differently. It was exciting to see how the rest of the world lived.

I had been around other races, but not blacks. I'd been raised, of course, in the San Joaquin Valley, around Armenians and Japanese and Mexicans and other people who were not caucasian, but I had never known any blacks. I just thought everyone was an individual. Before I met McMillan, I'd taken in a roommate named Everleen Ford. She happened to be black, but I just thought nothing at all about it. We worked together, and I guess I was accustomed to Everleen. We worked so hard and such long hours that I really didn't have much time, except for flying, to do other things, and we didn't do much together; I really didn't think of her as black, either.

McMillan and I got married on June 20, 1964. He wanted to get married on a Saturday night to conform with ethnic tradition—he said that's the night when people go out and celebrate. When we started talking about getting a marriage license he wanted to go over to the marriage license bureau about midnight, and that struck me as strange. Why would anybody want to go at twelve o'clock to get a marriage license? Well, it was so nobody would be around to see a black man with a white woman, because there was a miscegenation law that said that blacks and whites could not marry. Mac used to be very, very careful. We would drive to Los Angeles so he could attend the conferences of the Urban League, and he was always very careful about where we would stay and about getting a reservation. (He used to kid me about the federal "white slavery" law and transporting white women over state lines.) I understood why he thought he had to be so cautious, but I didn't believe it was necessary.

McMillan's previous wife had friends in the black community, and he didn't want me to have the same friends and the same experiences. Of course, I was always busy working, so the only time that I would meet black people and his friends was when we'd go to meetings or social events or something, and I never had any problem. I didn't know them very well, and I didn't have much time to spend in the black community, actually. I didn't have much free time to pursue anything like that. I can remember the first political club that I joined—it was a women's Democratic club, and the majority of the members were Afro-Americans. At that time we wore hats and gloves and things, and the women were very pleasant and very accepting of me. Now that I look back on it, I suppose they didn't have any choice, but I loved to meet them and they loved to meet me.

McMillan would get threats. People would call him and threaten him, and I got a few calls at the house. They'd say, "Stay away from that nigger," you know. "What are you doing with that black guy?" I'd just hang up. McMillan would say, "Don't worry, don't pay any attention to it," but he would get calls at the office that concerned him. He would tell me, "Now, I want you to take care because I had a call today." He might say, "I want you to be careful about starting the car," or something like that. He's always done most of his NAACP business at the office, and he would get these calls. Then the car of my attorney, Bill Coulthard, was blown up, and after that I was very concerned for myself and began to be afraid that someone would do something. My brother, Jim Stever, taught me how to check my car before starting it. I still do.

After we'd been married a while, people just accepted us, I guess. We did things that everybody wanted to do, but nobody did but us. We always drove sports cars, and we were both pilots, and we took a lot of trips to interesting places. We'd fly everywhere; we'd fly down to Cabo San Lucas for weekends, to Catalina Island, to Acapulco, the Bahamas . . . . We went everywhere and did everything we wanted to do, and after our son Jeff was born we always took him with us —I would never leave him. So we did all of these things, and everybody just loved to hear what we did and how and where we did it.

After about ten years or so of marriage, I started getting a different sort of call—calls from both white and black women about mixed marriages. Young people wanting to get married, and they had heard about our marriage . . . young women wanting to know if I had had any problems, and asking me to advise them whether or not they should get married. Then I really knew that we had something different. And it *was* different. The first time one called, I said, "How did you get my name?" She said, "Well, I was down at the

"After we had been married awhile, people just accepted us,
I guess."

funeral home, and they said I should give you a call. I am very much in love with this black man, and everybody tells me that I have to be careful." I told her to follow her heart. I did what my heart told me to do, and I've had the most wonderful marriage that anybody could have. I kept thinking that they would call me back later to tell me what had happened, but I never heard from any of them again.

In 1969 we went back to Nashville to attend the twenty-fifth anniversary reunion of McMillan's graduating class at Meharry Medical College. We also spent a day in Memphis just so he could show me the deep South. He said, "I want you to know." He wanted me to see how they had had separate drinking fountains . . . all the apparatus of segregation. And I saw "sugar hill." That was where affluent white people lived, and when blacks made it professionally or financially, they moved to "sugar hill."

Even after we married I did not spend much time on the Westside, but McMillan knew very interesting black people all over the country, and the people I saw at meetings in Los Angeles, San Francisco, Atlanta, Detroit, Nashville, and who came to visit us in Las Vegas were all educated people, professionals. We fit right in with them, and I loved all of them. We just got along famously. Things have changed in the last thirty-five years: now there are many black professional people in Las Vegas, but there were only a few back then.

When we married in 1964, each of us had two children from previous marriages. Then we had a son together in 1966, Jeffrey Bernard McMillan. All McMillan's children were JBMs. His name is James Bates McMillan, and he named his first son James Bates McMillan, and his daughter was Jarmilla Bernadette McMillan. So when we had a son, he had to be a JB. Our kids never had any problems due to our interracial marriage that I knew about. Of course we always lived in the same house and they went to the same schools. Perhaps Jeff has had a few problems, but he hasn't talked about them to me. He may have talked to his dad when I wasn't around.

When we were first married, the civil rights struggle occupied a large part of McMillan's life. He handled most of it from his office, but he didn't keep me out of it, and as we had people come over I became more and more aware of what was happening. I'd be there when he and Dave Hoggard were planning how they were going to do things, and I'd try to interject my thoughts. I don't know how much they listened to me—at the time they thought that only blacks should have a say in these things. (Of course, any meetings they had with the mayor or anybody else in power *had* to be integrated if they were going to get anything done.) They didn't listen to me on the bank issue, and I think they were not successful because they wouldn't accept my advice.

After the Moulin Rouge agreement, McMillan very much wanted to start a bank to be controlled by blacks. He wanted black entrepreneurs and businessmen to have access to capital—a black bank and savings and loan company would ensure that they wouldn't be discriminated against through redlining, which had occurred in so many other institutions. But after you get a charter you have to raise so much money to open a bank, and I suggested that he make it an integrated bank. He said, "This needs to be controlled by blacks." Well, it's impossible to raise that much money without getting whites involved, so in the end the stockholders were integrated, but the bank never happened. There have been several other things that I've seen go that same way. When you have black pride, you want to ensure that your people are protected, but it won't work without integration. I would say to him, "Look, you and I are integrated. Isn't this good?"

"Oh yes, but that's not the same."

It *is* the same, and I still think so. But he still thinks his way is best.

Over the years Mac's taken at least five other dentists into his dental office to relieve the burden of his practice so he could get some time off; but instead, he stays there and they take a vacation and he has to cover for them. So he never gets a vacation. Then they open their own practice, and he gives them half of his patients. Then his patients build up again because he's honest and is a good dentist, and he gets a full house again, so he'll take somebody else in. He works harder and harder, and I say, "Now's the time to quit." But he won't.

McMillan has the biggest, kindest heart of anyone I've ever met, except our son Jeff. He's a softy. But he's very strict with his family—he thinks it takes a strong father to make a good family. McMillan raised his first two children almost by himself, and he *had* to be involved. But there's a difference between how fathers get involved and how mothers get involved. When we were first married, James and Jeri were in high school, and I went to every debate that James was ever in. He was a tremendous debater—I can remember when he debated with Frankie Sue Del Papa, who is now our attorney general. I'd say, "McMillan, you have to come hear James speak." And he'd say, "No. Mothers do that." He had meetings planned and things to do . . . . He's a strong family man, but he thinks differently about his family than I do; there's just a difference. Perhaps it's the way we were brought up. He was brought up by his mother, who was a strong person, and I believe that he thought that as long as I was involved, I was the main person to take care of the family.

I was so proud of James B. at that time—he would introduce me to people as his mother. We were so close when he was in school, and I was so proud of him. Jeri graduated the year McMillan and I were married, and my friend Everleen and I designed and made her senior ball gown. It was pink and strapless, and I just tried to outdo myself to make the most beautiful senior ball gown that any young girl ever had.

Sometimes I don't think I'll ever get to what I want to tell you about. At that time, you see, we had to keep two houses . . . . We had the most terrific married life that anybody ever had, but we kept two houses for years. Mac was a very strong family man, but it was in a way that was different from the way most caucasians would think. It was different. And it appears to me now that this is different about black people. When we met, Mac lived on the Westside at 524 Wyatt, and I lived where we live now. His mother was sick with Parkinson's disease, and she and her husband lived with him and he supported them. Then when we married he moved in with me, and his mother and stepfather stayed in his house on Wyatt. My children were away at school in Europe, but his children were with him, and I wanted us all to live like a family; but he wanted one of his children to stay with Granny all of the time. That was just one of the stipulations he made—that was their duty. So they took turns staying with us: Jeri would stay with Granny for a while, and then James would stay with Granny for a while. But they didn't like to stay with Granny. I think they thought that I was the one that didn't want them with us, but I always wanted a large family. I loved children, especially them.

My children were named Jack and Michelle. Michelle died in an automobile accident at age twenty-four in Connecticut. She was Mac's favorite; he was just crazy about her. She had an IQ in the genius class, she was a swimmer, and I don't know . . . he and Michelle just hit it off and he always loved her. She was going to be a linguist. She went to school in Switzerland, and she spoke French, Italian, and Spanish, and she could pick up languages easily. Jeff speaks Spanish and has that talent also. When he was born I was forty years old and McMillan was almost fifty, and we discussed many times how unfortunate it was that we weren't married earlier, because I think we might have had twelve children. He would have liked that also, and we would have had a strong family, because I would have been a strong mother. I always insisted that we all have dinner together, and we would talk and discuss books and people and travel and things like that. But one of his children always had to stay with Granny.

Mac was a strong father and he took care of disciplining James and Jeri. He was always very strict with them. I guess he thought he had to be because I wasn't so strict. He'd been through all of this civil rights stuff, trying to raise children at the same time, so they hadn't had an ideal home life. I could see that, and I tried to make up for it. Mac wanted them to go to church, be clean, go to school; but other things, like saving . . . . Mac was pretty easy with money. I've heard people tell him, "You wouldn't have a dime to your name if it weren't for Marie," but McMillan and I've put money in lots of things that went bad. We spent more money than most people ever earn in their whole lives. We've thrown it away, given it away, loaned it and done fun things with it, and we could die tomorrow and we wouldn't care.

Mac likes independent women. Of course, he knows I will always do and say the right thing; he's sure of that, so he lets me do what I want and he supports every one of my projects. But he's a male chauvinist. Although he loves his home, he would never do anything *around* the home. He has no idea whatsoever what that consists of. He's always busy, always has meetings, and he simply doesn't have time; and he knows I'll do it or call someone to have it done. I've never asked him to lift a hand. Mac's just from another era. On the other hand, people think I'm the luckiest woman in the entire world because I can do anything I want and he is very encouraging. They'll say, "Well, my husband won't let me do that."

Together, we made a formidable team. McMillan had these forward-thinking plans and he could predict how they would or could affect the situation. I, in turn, could

Above: Christmas 1967, Marie holding Jeff, flanked by Michelle (l.) and Jeri (r.). Below: Jack (holding Jeff) and James, 1968.

carry out projects, write, and take care of the details and paperwork. One such project was our acquisition of land for farming in California. Mac had gone there with his football team in college, and he'd seen the orange groves, fruit trees and farm land and told himself that one day he would own some. When we would fly over to visit my family, we began to acquire orchards and raw land in plots that were adjacent to one another, and eventually we ended up with a large farm. Managing the farm became my job.

One time we bought an orange grove that was next to some land that we owned. In the center of the grove was a lake with an island in the middle. Pine trees grew on it, and we called it Christmas Tree Island. There was a small cabin on it which became the center of operations for our properties, and that was where I stayed. We developed our acreage and planted over ten varieties of plums, two varieties of nectarines and two varieties of oranges. Eventually we had so much fruit that it became difficult to transport it to an outside packing house, so our son, Jack, took a year off to help me develop and build a packing house on the property. After that, McMillan Ranches packed their own fruit. This was just one of the ideas that McMillan tried.

McMillan has to be the greatest man I have ever known, and the expression, "born thirty years too soon" is 100 percent accurate in describing him. When I first met him, I could see that he wanted something bigger than most of us can even envision. He still does. He's still very concerned about civil rights and improving the lives of black people in this country, but he has been frustrated by the slow pace of change. Many of the hopes and ideas that he had for his people more than thirty years ago, and the ways to implement them, are just now being tried and going into effect. He was just born too soon for his time. Few people think like he does now—most just aren't concerned about what's going to happen to blacks and other minorities. That saddens him. If McMillan doesn't do it, I don't know who will; and he doesn't have the time left to do it.

Index

W

Fighting Back

Camera-ready master composed and printed
at the University of Nevada Oral History Program
in Bauer Bodoni, using WordPerfect 6.1 for Windows
and a Hewlett Packard LaserJet IIISi printer.